EDUCATION AND TRAINI.

No More Failures: Ten Steps to Equity in Education

by

Simon Field, Małgorzata Kuczera, Beatriz Pont

OECD

ORGANISATION FOR ECONOMIC CO-OPERATION AND DEVELOPMENT

The OECD is a unique forum where the governments of 30 democracies work together to address the economic, social and environmental challenges of globalisation. The OECD is also at the forefront of efforts to understand and to help governments respond to new developments and concerns, such as corporate governance, the information economy and the challenges of an ageing population. The Organisation provides a setting where governments can compare policy experiences, seek answers to common problems, identify good practice and work to co-ordinate domestic and international policies.

The OECD member countries are: Australia, Austria, Belgium, Canada, the Czech Republic, Denmark, Finland, France, Germany, Greece, Hungary, Iceland, Ireland, Italy, Japan, Korea, Luxembourg, Mexico, the Netherlands, New Zealand, Norway, Poland, Portugal, the Slovak Republic, Spain, Sweden, Switzerland, Turkey, the United Kingdom and the United States. The Commission of the European Communities takes part in the work of the OECD.

OECD Publishing disseminates widely the results of the Organisation's statistics gathering and research on economic, social and environmental issues, as well as the conventions, guidelines and standards agreed by its members.

This work is published on the responsibility of the Secretary-General of the OECD. The opinions expressed and arguments employed herein do not necessarily reflect the official views of the Organisation or of the governments of its member countries.

Also available in French under the title:
En finir avec l'échec scolaire : Dix mesures pour une éducation équitable

Foreword

There is growing attention to the issue of equity in education. Mass expansion in education systems was linked to a wave of optimism that it would enable young people, regardless of background, to achieve their full potential. If much has been achieved, there has also been much disappointment. The spotlight of OECD's PISA assessments reminds us that in many countries an unacceptably large number of young people are failing to acquire basic skills. No More Failures sets out a challenge to failure, both in individual learners and in education systems, and advances ten steps in an agenda for enhancing equity in education.

The book is based on an OECD study on equity in education, but it also draws on evidence from across the OECD. The ten participant countries each prepared an analytical background report, and in five countries an OECD team of experts conducted a review visit and produced a report with policy recommendations. All these reports are available on the OECD website at www.oecd.org/edu/equity/equityineducation.

No More Failures argues that equity in education is a key objective of education systems and that it needs to be addressed on three fronts: the design of education systems, educational practices and resourcing. The book is designed to be accessible to busy people. The ten steps are set out in a single page at the outset, then expanded – but still in summary form – to provide the key supporting evidence. The detailed report follows.

The authors are indebted to the countries who took part in the study, to delegates of other countries, to the expert teams who participated in the country visits and provided invaluable comments on the report, and to OECD colleagues in the Directorate for Education and the Directorate for Employment, Labour and Social Affairs. Our particular thanks to Susan Copeland for her role in preparing the final text and to Christine Mercier for the French translation.

Table of contents

The Ten Steps... 9

Executive Summary... 11

Chapter 1. Introduction: Setting the Agenda 25
    1.1. Why look at equity in education? 26
    1.2. Background to this study 27
    1.3. The context: equity as a public policy objective 29
    1.4. Why equity in education?................................ 31
    References 34

Chapter 2. A Look at Inequities in Education 37
    2.1. Unequal improvements in educational attainment........... 38
    2.2. Equity as fairness....................................... 41
    2.3. Equity as inclusion...................................... 44
    2.4. The two dimensions of equity overlap 48
    2.5. Policy implications 50
    References.. 52

Chapter 3. Structures and Pathways 55
    3.1. Differentiation in schooling structures and the risks to equity . 56
    3.2. Early tracking and comprehensive schooling 65
    3.3. Designing an inclusive upper secondary education system 67
    3.4. Removing dead ends and providing second chances.......... 74
    3.5. Summary conclusions and recommendations 78
    Annex 3.A1. Correlation coefficients between separation index
              and PISA outcomes................................ 81
    Annex 3.A2. Regression analysis: Effects of selection by ability
              on different measures 81
    Notes 82
    References.. 82

Chapter 4. School and Out-of-school Practices 87
    4.1. Equity in the classroom: interventions for those in need 88
    4.2. Schools reaching out to homes 99
    4.3. Home influence on school performance 101
    4.4. Summary conclusions and recommendations 106
    References.. 108

Chapter 5. Resources and Outcomes 111
    5.1. Allocating resources across educational sectors. 112
    5.2. Allocating resources across individuals, institutions and regions 121
    5.3. Defining outcomes to take account of equity 126
    5.4. Summary conclusions and recommendations 132
    References 134

Chapter 6. Groups at Risk: The Special Case of Migrants and Minorities . . 139
    6.1. The migration context. 140
    6.2. Immigrant disadvantage in education 143
    6.3. Policy interventions 147
    6.4. Summary conclusions and recommendations 150
    Notes 151
    References 152

List of Boxes

    1.1. OECD Thematic Review on Equity in Education. 27
    1.2. Two dimensions of equity in education 29
    1.3. Recognising equity and inequity 31
    1.4. Equity in the knowledge economy. 32
    3.1. Who knows how things would have turned out? 68
    3.2. Parallel secondary education completion programmes
        in selected countries 69
    3.3. The Early College High School Initiative in the United States 70
    3.4. VET Reforms to improve equity and quality. 72
    3.5. Adult learning institutions in different countries 75
    3.6. Work-based learning initiatives for the employed
        and the unemployed 76
    4.1. An alternative approach to year repetition in France. 93
    4.2. Tackling learning difficulties in Finland 97
    4.3. The teaching profession in Finland 99
    4.4. Developing learning communities. 105
    5.1. Directing resources to disadvantaged schools in France, Ireland
        and Belgium. 125
    5.2. Targets for equity in education 127
    5.3. The impact of high stakes schools testing in the United States . . . 129
    5.4. Different approaches to reporting of school-level tests across
        OECD countries 131
    6.1. Should data be collected on ethnic minorities? 142
    6.2. Swedish programme for Roma children 148

NO MORE FAILURES: TEN STEPS TO EQUITY IN EDUCATION – ISBN 978-92-64-03259-0 – © OECD

List of Tables

3.1.   Selection and school choice practices   61
3.2.   Selected approaches to recognition of prior learning   77
4.1.   Year repetition in primary and lower secondary education   89
4.2.   Estimated costs of year repetition in selected countries   92
5.1.   Public financial support for students in compulsory
       and post-compulsory school (without tertiary)   116
6.1.   Language training for children with immigrant background
       in basic education.   147
6.2.   Language training for adult immigrants.   149

List of Figures

1.1.   Income inequality varies across OECD   30
2.1.   Younger people have higher levels of education.   39
2.2.   Women moving ahead?   40
2.3.   How social background affects performance in mathematics   41
2.4.   Attainment and the social mix in schools   43
2.5.   The well-qualified make most use of adult education   44
2.6.   How many continue and how many drop out at different levels
       of education?   45
2.7.   Getting a good start in life.   47
2.8.   How many students struggle with reading?   48
2.9.   How many leave education before the end of upper secondary
       school?   49
2.10. Weaker performance by immigrant students (2003).   50
3.1.   Social sorting between schools.   57
3.2.   Where attainment determines the school attended   58
3.3.   Does school choice increase social differences between
       schools? (2003)   64
3.4.   Some countries with larger VET systems have lower dropout
       rates (2001, 2002).   71
4.1.   How many students repeat years in primary and lower
       secondary school?.   90
4.2.   How home circumstances affect school performance   100
4.3.   Learning time in and out of school (2003).   103
5.1.   Spending rises as students progress (2003)   114
5.2.   Universities or schools? Funding priorities   115
5.3.   Starting strong: big returns from early childhood education.   118
5.4.   Where education spending goes (2003)   120
5.5.   Regional variations in education spending: the example of Spain   123
5.6.   Construction spending on public schools in the United States. . . .   123
6.1.   Immigrant populations and their educational attainment
       (2002, 2004).   141

ISBN 978-92-64-03259-0
No More Failures: Ten Steps to Equity in Education
© OECD 2007

The Ten Steps

Policy Recommendations for Equity in Education

This report argues that education systems need to be fair and inclusive in their design, practices, and resourcing. It advances ten steps – major policy recommendations – which would reduce school failure and dropout, make society fairer and avoid the large social costs of marginalised adults with few basic skills.

Design

1. Limit early tracking and streaming and postpone academic selection.

2. Manage school choice so as to contain the risks to equity.

3. In upper secondary education, provide attractive alternatives, remove dead ends and prevent dropout.

4. Offer second chances to gain from education.

Practices

5. Identify and provide systematic help to those who fall behind at school and reduce year repetition.

6. Strengthen the links between school and home to help disadvantaged parents help their children to learn.

7. Respond to diversity and provide for the successful inclusion of migrants and minorities within mainstream education.

Resourcing

8. Provide strong education for all, giving priority to early childhood provision and basic schooling.

9. Direct resources to students and regions with the greatest needs.

10. Set concrete targets for more equity, particularly related to low school attainment and dropouts.

The report advances recommendations on priorities for spending within a limited budget, allowing for public expenditure constraints. Actual costs or savings arising from these recommendations have not been estimated, as they will depend on national contexts.

Executive Summary

Introduction

Defining equity in education

Equity in education has two dimensions. The first is *fairness*, which implies ensuring that personal and social circumstances – for example gender, socio-economic status or ethnic origin – should not be an obstacle to achieving educational potential. The second is *inclusion*, which implies ensuring a basic minimum standard of education for all – for example that everyone should be able to read, write and do simple arithmetic. The two dimensions are closely intertwined: tackling school failure helps to overcome the effects of social deprivation which often causes school failure.

Why does equity in education matter?

The benefits from education are large. In the United States, for example, workers with tertiary qualifications earn more than double the income of those with no post-compulsory qualifications. Education is associated with better health, a longer life, successful parenting and civic participation. Fair and inclusive education is one of the most powerful levers available to make society more equitable.

Fair and inclusive education is desirable because:

- There is a human rights imperative for people to be able to develop their capacities and participate fully in society. The right to education is recognised, for example, in the United Nations Declaration of the Rights of the Child and in the constitution of most nations.

- The long-term social and financial costs of educational failure are high. Those without the skills to participate socially and economically generate higher costs for health, income support, child welfare and security.

- Increased migration poses new challenges for social cohesion in some countries while other countries face long-standing issues of integrating minorities. Fair and inclusive education for migrants and minorities is a key to these challenges. Equity in education enhances social cohesion and trust.

Is education a friend to equity?

● In the past half-century education has expanded, but hopes that this would bring about a fairer society have been only partly realised. Women have made dramatic advances (see Figure 2.2), but social mobility has not risen overall and inequalities of income and wealth have increased in some places.

● The general upgrading of qualifications has highlighted the position of those who have not shared in this advance. Many adults remain unqualified and some young people still do not successfully complete secondary education. Across the OECD nearly one in three adults (30%) have only primary or lower secondary education – a real disadvantage in terms of employment and life chances

Women moving ahead? (Figure 2.2, Chapter 2)
Difference between men and women in number of years spent in formal education, for two different age groups (2004)

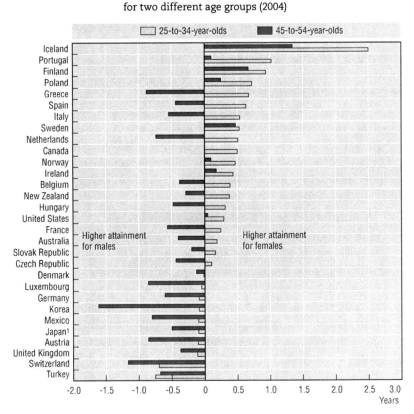

1. Year of reference 2003.
Source: OECD (2006), *Education at a Glance: OECD Indicators 2006*, OECD, Paris.

NO MORE FAILURES: TEN STEPS TO EQUITY IN EDUCATION – ISBN 978-92-64-03259-0 – © OECD

Where are the big problems?

Figure 2.3 illustrates the problem of *unfairness*. It shows that in most OECD countries children from poorer homes are between three and four times more likely to be in the lowest scoring group in mathematics at age 15.

How social background affects performance in mathematics (Figure 2.3, Chapter 2)

Relative chances of students in lowest and highest socio-economic group ending up with very poor (below or at Level 1) performance in mathematics (2003)

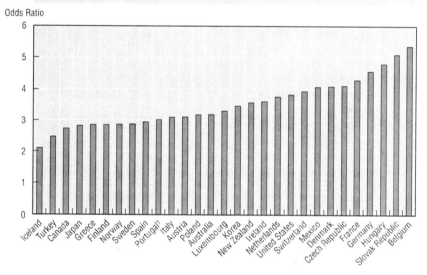

1. For example, in Portugal a student with low SES is three times more likely to be a low mathematics achiever than a student with high SES.

Source: OECD (2006), *Education at a Glance: OECD Indicators 2006*, OECD, Paris.

Figure 2.8 illustrates the problem of lack of *inclusion*. It shows how many students struggle with reading in OECD countries and how many risk leaving school without basic skills for work and life in the 21st century. Significantly, it also shows that there are big differences between countries.

There are three policy domains which may bear on equity in education: the *design* of education systems (covered in Chapter 3), *practices* in and out of school (Chapter 4) and *resourcing* (Chapter 5). Chapter 6, which examines the special case of migrants and minorities, also contains policy recommendations on practices. Within these domains, we advance ten steps – major policy recommendations – to enhance equity in education.

13

How many students struggle with reading? (Figure 2.8, Chapter 2)[1]

Percentage of students below and at Level 1 of proficiency in the OECD PISA reading scale[2] (2003)

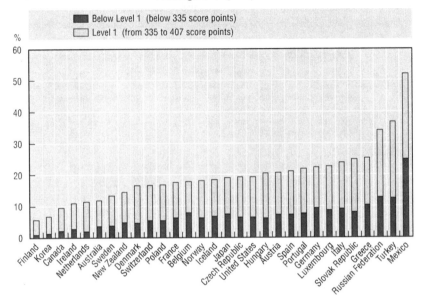

1. Countries are ranked in descending order of percentage of 15-year-olds in Levels 2, 3, 4, 5 and 6.
2. The PISA scale has six levels of proficiency. Level 2 represents the baseline at which students begin having skills that allow them to use reading actively. Level 1 and below imply insufficient reading skills to function in today's societies.

Source: OECD (2004), *Learning for Tomorrow's World: First Results from PISA 2003*, OECD, Paris.

Steps 1 to 4: Design for fair and inclusive education (Chapter 3)

The structure of education systems and the pathways through them can help or hinder equity. Traditionally, education systems have sorted students into different tracks, institutions and streams according to attainment. This sorting sometimes increases inequalities and inequities.

Step1: Limit early tracking and streaming and postpone academic selection

Evidence

● Secondary school systems with large social differences between schools tend on average to have worse results in mathematics and reading and a greater spread of reading outcomes. Social background is more of an obstacle to educational success than in systems where there are not large socio-economic differences between schools.

● Academic selection by school systems is associated with great social differences between schools and a stronger effect of socio-economic status

NO MORE FAILURES: TEN STEPS TO EQUITY IN EDUCATION – ISBN 978-92-64-03259-0 – © OECD 2

on performance, but also with a stronger performance at the top end of the scale in mathematics and science.

- Evidence on secondary students from PISA (OECD's Programme for International Student Assessment) compared to evidence at primary level from PIRLS (Progress in International Reading Literacy Study) and evidence from countries which have introduced comprehensive schooling suggest that early tracking is associated with reduced equity in outcomes and sometimes weakens results overall.

Policy recommendations

- *Early tracking and streaming* need to be justified in terms of proven benefits as they very often pose risks to equity.
- School systems using *early tracking* should consider raising the age of first tracking to reduce inequities and improve outcomes.
- *Academic selection* needs to be used with caution since it too poses risks to equity.

Step 2: Manage school choice so as to contain the risks to equity

Evidence

- School choice may pose risks to equity since well-educated parents may make shrewder choices. Better-off parents have the resources to exploit choice, and academic selection tends to accelerate the progress of those who have already gained the best start in life from their parents.
- Across countries, greater choice in school systems is associated with larger differences in the social composition of different schools (see Figure 3.3).

Policy recommendations

- *School choice poses risks to equity* and requires careful management, in particular to ensure that it does not result in increased differences in the social composition of different schools.
- Given school choice, oversubscribed schools need ways to *ensure an even social mix in schools* – for example, selection methods such as lottery arrangements. Financial premiums to schools attracting disadvantaged pupils may also help.

Step 3: In upper secondary education, provide attractive alternatives, remove dead ends and prevent dropout

Evidence

- Between 5% and 40% of students drop out of school in OECD countries (measured by the proportion of 20-to-24-year-olds not in education and

**Does school choice increase the social differences between schools? (2003)
(Figure 3.3, Chapter 3)**

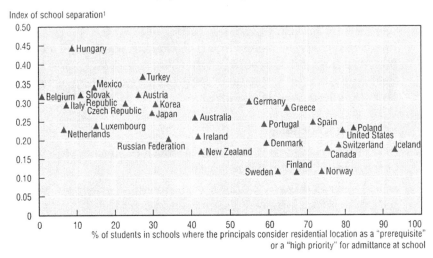

1. The index of separation shows the extent to which a country has sorted children (15-year-olds) from different socio-economic backgrounds into different schools, with zero representing a country in which all schools have a similar social composition. The index is developed with the ESCS, the PISA index of economic, social and cultural status. See Annex A1 in OECD (2004), *Learning for Tomorrow's World: First Results from PISA 2003*, Paris.

Source: OECD (2004), *Learning for Tomorrow's World: First Results from PISA 2003*, OECD, Paris.

without upper secondary education). They go on to have low skills and suffer high rates of unemployment.

● Among other factors, dropout stems from disenchantment with school, lack of support at home, negative learning experiences and repeating years.

● Early identification of students at risk helps to improve outcomes and prevent dropout.

● Good career guidance and counselling combined with a more flexible and diverse (and therefore attractive) curriculum help to reduce dropout rates.

Policy recommendations

● *Early prevention* of dropout is the best cure. Basic schooling should support and engage those who struggle at school as well as those who excel.

● *Monitoring* of those at risk (using information on attendance, performance and involvement in school activities) should be linked to interventions to improve outcomes and prevent dropout.

● *Upper secondary education* needs to be attractive not just to an academically inclined elite, offering good quality pathways without dead ends and effective links to the world of work.

- *Smooth transitions* prevent school failure and dropout. Additional learning support at the end of secondary school may help to encourage students to stay in school.

- *Good quality vocational tracks* are essential. Removing an academic hurdle from entrance to general upper secondary education and allowing access to tertiary education from vocational programmes, as Sweden and Norway have done, can increase the status of the vocational track.

The well-qualified make most use of adult education (Figure 2.5, Chapter 2)

Relative chances of adults with tertiary education participating in adult learning compared to those with only primary education (2003)

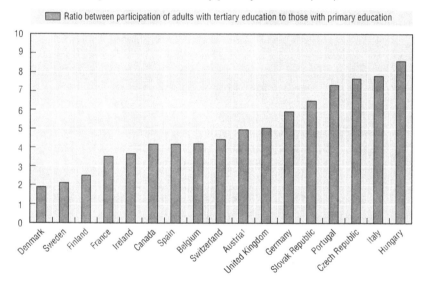

1. For example, in Austria a university graduate is five times more likely to participate in adult learning than an adult with primary education.

Source: European Labour Force Survey, 2003.

Step 4: Offer second chances to gain from education

Evidence

- Those who fail at school often find it difficult to recover later on. In all OECD countries, those with weak basic qualifications are much less likely to continue learning in adult life (see Figure 2.5). Significantly, this figure also shows that there are big differences between countries.

- Across OECD countries, many adults and young dropouts without basic education obtain school qualifications through second chance programmes. In the United States, almost 60% of dropouts eventually earn a high school credential (GED certificate).

Policy recommendations

- *Second chances are necessary* for those who lack basic education and skills. These include programmes that provide literacy training, primary and secondary education, work-based programmes, and arrangements to recognise informal learning.

Steps 5 to 7: Fair and inclusive practices (Chapters 4 and 6)

Practices in the classroom affect equity as do out-of-school practices, particularly relationships between schools, parents and communities. Student learning benefits from an effective school-home relationship, but children from deprived backgrounds may not benefit if they have weak support at home. Effective provision for migrants and minorities in the education system is also a key challenge for equity.

Step 5: Identify and provide systematic help to those who fall behind at school and reduce high rates of school-year repetition

Evidence

- In some school systems, up to one-quarter of students repeat a year at some point. In others it is rare. Some countries, such as Luxembourg, are taking steps to reduce the extent of repetition.

- Although year repetition is often popular with teachers, there is little evidence that children gain benefit from it. Repetition is expensive – the full economic cost is up to USD 20 000 equivalent for each student who repeats a year – but schools have few incentives to take into account the costs involved.

- The classroom is the first level of intervention for equity. Evidence shows that it is possible to improve classroom attainment with methods such as formative assessment – a process of feeding back information about performance to student and teacher and adapting and improving teaching and learning in response, particularly with students at risk.

- "Reading recovery" strategies – short-term, intensive interventions of one-on-one lessons – can help many poor readers to catch up.

- Finland uses a hierarchy of successive formal and informal interventions to assist those falling behind at school. This approach appears to be successful: only 1% of 15-year-olds are unable to demonstrate basic functional reading skills, while the OECD average is 7%.

Policy recommendations

- *High rates of year repetition in some countries need to be reduced* by changing incentives for schools and encouraging alternative approaches.

- *Interventions in the classroom* can be very effective in tackling underachievement. Among the approaches available, we can highlight formative assessment, reading recovery strategies and careful monitoring.

- **Many** countries could usefully follow *the successful Finnish approach to learning difficulties*, offering a sequence of intensifying interventions which draw back into the mainstream those who fall behind.

- *Teaching professionals should have support to develop their in-classroom techniques* to help those in the class who are falling behind.

Step 6: Strengthen the links between school and home to help disadvantaged parents help their children to learn

Evidence

- On average, children in OECD countries spend more than 20% of their total learning time out of school – doing homework, working with a tutor or on other activities.

- Home factors, including parental support for education, engagement with children's learning and cultural assets (like books) are associated with stronger school performance.

- Homework can improve school outcomes, but reliance on homework may also threaten equity, since some children lack the home support necessary to realise its benefits.

- Parental involvement – working with children at home and actively participating in school activities – does improve results. All other things being equal, schools that foster communication and participation by parents, and encourage and assist parents to support their children with their school work tend to have better outcomes.

Policy recommendations

- To support learning among disadvantaged children, schools need to target their efforts to *improve communication with parents* in the most disadvantaged homes and help develop home environments conducive to learning.

- *After-school homework clubs* at school may also provide an environment that supports homework for those with weak home support.

Step 7: Respond to diversity and provide for the successful inclusion of migrants and minorities within mainstream education

Evidence

- Success in both education and employment varies widely between immigrant and minority groups and between different countries.

- Minority groups are, in many cases, less likely than others to participate in early childhood education and care, more likely to be in special education and more likely to drop out or end up in low status tracks and streams.

- For some "visible minority" groups, labour market discrimination is sometimes extensive. This limits employment prospects and reduces the incentives to obtain qualifications.

- In most countries, immigrant students of first and second generation tend to perform less well than their native counterparts in the PISA assessments of mathematics, science and reading, while second-generation students tend to outperform first-generation students. Analysis suggests that much but not all of this is explained by social background factors.

Policy recommendations

- *Early childhood education and care* is helpful for disadvantaged children and provides a strong environment in which to learn a second language. Special measures may encourage participation by the children of immigrants.

- Where immigrant and minority groups are *disproportionately streamed into special education institutions*, attention needs to be given to a) the risk of cultural bias in the diagnosis and b) whether separate schooling is in the best interests of the students involved.

- Newly arrived immigrant children often need *special language training*, but funding mechanisms and the approach selected to deliver this training should not encourage the isolation of such children from mainstream classes after an initial period of at most one year.

- Particularly in countries where immigration has risen sharply, teachers need *professional development* to deal with new demands on matters such as second language learning, a multicultural curriculum and teaching for tolerance and antiracism.

Steps 8 to 10: Fair and inclusive resourcing (Chapter 5)

In many countries, aggregate increases in educational expenditure will be hard to justify in terms of their contribution to equity, although they may contribute to economic growth. This highlights the importance of targeting education expenditure – both across education sectors and across regions and institutions – to ensure that it contributes to equity. National targets for equity outcomes can help.

NO MORE FAILURES: TEN STEPS TO EQUITY IN EDUCATION – ISBN 978-92-64-03259-0 – © OECD 2

Step 8: Provide strong education for all, giving priority to early childhood provision and basic schooling

Evidence

- Public provision of education can foster equity when it counterbalances poor home circumstances at the outset of children's lives. But it may increase inequity when it provides a common resource harvested by those who are best prepared for it.

- Education expenditure is shifting between sectors in many countries; in some the expansion of tertiary education is a large expenditure pressure. While countries need a high quality well-resourced tertiary education system, public expenditure on tertiary education tends to be regressive. Private sources can be tapped to fund this sector.

- Good quality affordable early childhood education and care has large long-term benefits, particularly for disadvantaged children.

- Grants to poor families for school-age children may reduce dropout at upper secondary level.

Starting strong: big returns from early childhood education (Figure 5.3, Chapter 5)

The Perry Preschool study: the impact of early childhood education and care as measured in two randomised samples

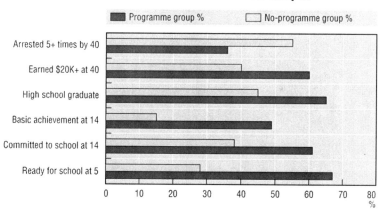

Source: OECD (2006), *Starting Strong II: Early Childhood Education and Care*, OECD, Paris, Figure 5.1.

Policy recommendations

- There is strong evidence that *early childhood education and care*, alongside public policy measures to improve the lives of young children, is the highest equity priority. If fees for early childhood education and care are applied at all, they should be moderate and remitted for those too poor to pay.

- *Basic education* remains an equity priority because it includes the entire cohort. Within this sector, particular attention should be given to efforts to sustain the performance of those with learning difficulties.

- When budgets are limited, public expenditure on *tertiary education will rarely be an equity priority*. Countries charging fees for early childhood education and care but not for tertiary education need to review their policies.

- Countries where *grants to families for school age children* are tied to school performance need to review their policies, since this may in fact encourage dropout.

Regional variations in education spending: the example of Spain (Figure 5.5, Chapter 5)

Public expenditure on education (other than universities) in Spain
and in two autonomous communities of Spain, with the highest and lowest spending
on education per student

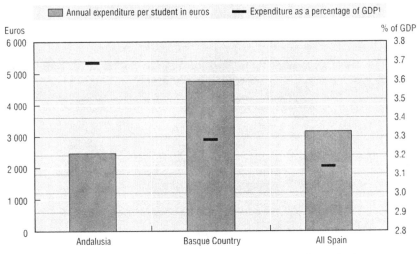

1. In Andalusia and Basque Country, expenditure as a percentage of GDP in the autonomous communities.

Source: Teese, R., S. Field, B. Pont (2005), *Equity in Education Thematic Review: Spain Country Note*, OECD, Paris; Calero, J. (2005), *Equity in Education Thematic Review: Country Analytical Report – Spain*.

Step 9: Direct resources to students and regions with the greatest needs

Evidence

- Within countries, regional autonomy in spending may cause disparities in the level of provision, unless it is balanced by mechanisms to redistribute resources to poorer regions.

- Many countries have special schemes to direct additional resources to schools or school areas serving disadvantaged pupils. Such schemes need to ensure that the extra resources are used to assist those most in need and avoid labelling certain schools as "disadvantaged", which may discourage students, teachers and parents.

● In many countries, less experienced teachers are working in "difficult" schools.

Policy recommendations

● Countries need adequate mechanisms to *redistribute resources and minimise regional inequities* of provision, so that minimum standards are met everywhere.

● *Extra resources* need to be channelled through schools to help disadvantaged students. This should help overcome the disadvantaging effect of social background, help to tackle poor performance without rewarding it and discourage schools from "selecting out" children from disadvantaged backgrounds. The stigma arising from labelling of particular schools as "for disadvantaged children" should be avoided.

● Experienced teachers are an important resource for disadvantaged schools. There should be *incentives* for them to work in these schools.

Step 10: Set concrete targets for more equity – particularly related to low school attainment and dropout

Evidence

● Numerical targets can be a useful policy lever for equity in education, by articulating policy in terms of what is to be achieved rather than in terms of formal processes or laws. A number of countries have adopted targets for equity in education.

● International comparisons with the best performing countries suggest that some countries could significantly reduce the number of dropouts and students failing to acquire basic skills.

● National testing of individual student performance on basic skills is a fundamental tool to measure both individual performance and the performance of elements of the education system. But test results are limited in what they measure, and results for schools depend on school intake as well as school quality.

● Many countries believe that the publication of results at school level is desirable or politically and/or legally inevitable. A minority of countries are testing but seeking to avoid publication. Some countries are pursuing "value-added" measures of school quality which take account of school intake.

Policy recommendations

- Countries should consider adopting a small number of *numerical targets for equity*, particularly for reducing the number of school-leavers with poor basic skills and the number of early school dropouts.

- Education systems need to plan carefully how to manage and respond to the public debate which follows publication of school-level test results and give strong *support to those schools with weak results* – using the data to bring all schools up to a level, rather than allowing the pressures of league tables to polarise school quality.

NO MORE FAILURES: TEN STEPS TO EQUITY IN EDUCATION – ISBN 978-92-64-03259-0 – © OECD

ISBN 978-92-64-03259-0
No More Failures: Ten Steps to Equity in Education
© OECD 2007

Chapter 1

Introduction: Setting the Agenda

This chapter introduces the issue of equity in education and describes the methods of this study and the scope of this report. It addresses issues such as equity in compulsory education, early school leaving and the impact of different education pathways on equity, and argues that although these are very common problems, they can be, and have been, successfully tackled. The chapter refers to the philosophical discussion on equity and offers a simple definition of two main dimensions of equity in education: fairness (that social background should be no barrier to outcomes) and inclusion (a basic minimum standard of education for all). It then looks at the broader public policy context within which equity objectives are pursued and the evidence of trends in inequalities of income. The final section argues that equity in education is a fundamental policy objective.

1.1. Why look at equity in education?

In 2003, the Programme for International Student Assessment (PISA) found that across OECD countries, 8% of 15-year-olds had very poor reading skills (below PISA Level 1) – a blight on the lives of the millions of school-children involved. Poor basic skills mean less chance of a job, worse health, more criminality and a shorter life. Evidence shows that the risks are compounded for those from deprived backgrounds and those who receive weak schooling. It is a familiar story which generates many familiar responses. Some say that there will always be a proportion of failures in any group, always some losers, some dropouts, some no-goods, some who won't or can't make it – and that schools, teachers and even parents can't make much of a difference. They say that some will always fail, that large inequalities are an inevitable part of life and to think otherwise is simply unrealistic.

That is a dismal picture. But when it came to the test in Finland *virtually no* girls were found to be poor readers – only 0.3% of 15-year-old girls. Finnish boys did not do quite so well: 1.8% were poor readers. But that is still less than a fifth of the OECD average for boys. The reasons for these extraordinary outcomes have to do with schooling in Finland and will be described later in this report. But the scale of what can be achieved is evident. It is not just a question of small reductions; the example suggests that the problem can be largely solved.

Of course, not everyone can do well at school, but the goal of equity in education is to ensure that as many as possible do so – acquiring basic and further skills, fulfilling themselves as human beings, overcoming accidents of personal circumstances and home background. There is no inevitability to failure in education. In Finland, and through other initiatives in many different countries, school failure and dropout can be successfully tackled. There are a number of clear lessons, backed by evidence, which if applied throughout the OECD would improve the life chances of millions of disadvantaged people and avoid a huge and shameful waste of human potential. We have set out these lessons in this report in the form of *ten steps to equity in education*.

It should be said at once that some of these lessons are not new; many of them echo the findings of other published reports. We make no apology for that. Desirable policies cannot always be implemented immediately, not least because there are many political pressures on education systems, interest groups to satisfy, and practical issues of implementation to work through and resolve. But our aim here is to provide a set of principles for equity in education and an agenda for policy.

1.2. Background to this study

This report aims to draw policy lessons on how to improve equity in education using material from the countries involved in the OECD Thematic Review of Equity in Education (Box 1.1), but it is set in the wider context of OECD countries. It draws on analytical reports prepared by authorities in each country, country notes by OECD review teams and other relevant research.

Box 1.1. **OECD Thematic Review on Equity in Education**

The Thematic Review on Equity in Education involved two strands of work for its ten participants: Belgium (Flanders), Finland, France, Hungary, Norway, the Russian Federation, Slovenia, Spain, Sweden and Switzerland. Each country prepared an *analytical report* on equity in education; and, in a subset of participating countries, country visits by teams of experts led to the preparation of *country notes*.

The *analytical reports* describe each country's context and current equity situation, provide a profile of equity in education, examine causes and explanations, and explore the effectiveness of existing policies and potential policy solutions to problems.

Five of the participating countries (Finland, Hungary, Norway, Spain and Sweden) opted for a country visit. The objective of these visits was to assess policy by exploring the perspectives of different stakeholders and observing practice in specific institutional contexts. OECD review teams of experts conducted in-depth examinations of national policies and practices and prepared a *country note* containing evaluation and policy recommendations.

All documents are available at *www.oecd.org/edu/equity/equityineducation*.

This report focuses on the following issues, which participating countries highlighted as important equity challenges:

* *Equity in compulsory education:* Despite universal education, some fail at school. PISA revealed a complex pattern of international variability in results, with differences between schools and within schools. Also, the increase in a number of countries of private or publicly supported private schools is giving rise to concerns about school choice and its impact on equity.

- *Early school leaving*: The transition to upper secondary education and the level of dropouts at this stage of education is a significant challenge for education systems in some countries. In Spain, for example, only 57% of those over 16 continue into upper secondary, while the EU objective for 2010 is to raise completion rates to 85%.

- *Different educational pathways and how they might be having an impact on equity*: In some countries, vocational education is a weak option, and other alternatives may not allow re-entry into the education system.

- *Integration of migrants and minorities in the education system*: This phenomenon is of long-standing importance in a number of countries, but it is a new and growing issue for others, particularly European countries. In Hungary, the provision of good quality education to the Roma population was a key concern.

The report offers a comparative perspective on how different countries have responded to their equity in education challenges. It brings together the different policies and strategies adopted across a number of OECD countries to target equity issues, seeks to raise awareness of the problem of inequity and provide a coherent set of policy levers for action. At the same time it is selective, in that it explores a number of particular issues emerging from reviews of the countries concerned in this exercise. It therefore aims to add value to the existing literature both through its international scope and breadth, and through its depth on specific issues.

Because much existing OECD work on education bears on equity issues, this report makes use of the results of previous thematic reviews such as those on early childhood education, teacher policy, transition from school to work and adult learning, as well as the results of the various PISA studies. We have sought to avoid duplication with these and ongoing OECD thematic reviews including the review of tertiary education. The combined effect has been to give this exercise more of a focus on schools. Other OECD work covers the situation of students with special learning needs or with disabilities (OECD, 2004a), so limited attention has been given to this issue here.

This report also draws from a paper commissioned for this review (Levin, 2003), which provides an in-depth conceptual discussion of equity and policy in education and reviews the outcome of a range of previous OECD work in the field. Other recent reports deserve immediate recognition. First, the recent communication from the European Union Commission (Council of the European Union, 2006; Commission of the European Communities, 2006) has provided some very useful analysis and recommendations, bearing on similar themes. EU work on indicators of equity (Baye *et al.*, 2006) is also very relevant.

Chapter 1 describes the objectives of the study and the methods adopted. Chapter 2 provides a largely statistical snapshot of inequities in education, examining how educational attainment is distributed and how social background affects attainment. The remainder of the report concentrates on the three sets of policy levers which may be used to deliver equity in education: the *design* of education systems, in-school and out-of-school *practices*, and *resourcing*. Chapter 3 looks at design – the structure of the education system and pathways through it. Chapter 4 looks at practices in and out of school and the home-school environment. Chapter 5 looks at how resources can be prioritised and targeted with equity in mind. Chapter 6 examines one major set of groups at risk – migrants and minorities.

1.3. The context: equity as a public policy objective

Equity is different from equality. It is associated with broader ideas of justice and fairness, sometimes with "equality of opportunity" and sometimes with "equivalent treatment". There is a great deal of philosophical literature on this. This report will not add to that literature, but will instead work pragmatically with two dimensions of equity: *fairness* and *inclusion* (see Box 1.2).

Box 1.2. **Two dimensions of equity in education**

For the purposes of our study, equity in education includes two dimensions, fairness and inclusion:

- *Fairness* implies that personal and social circumstances such as gender, socio-economic status or ethnic origin should not be an obstacle to educational success.
- *Inclusion* implies a minimum standard of education for all.

There is a wider context of public policy concerned with equity and social protection. The development of OECD welfare mechanisms in the past half century shows how different countries approach equity. Some countries have tended to limit social protection to very disadvantaged groups – providing no more than a very basic safety net – while others have extended benefits to a wide range of groups in society. These approaches display a varying willingness to redistribute resources, and reflect different values placed on equality as opposed to other goals, such as economic growth or rewarding enterprise. However, what these systems nearly all have in common is that they have aimed to provide a basic network of social protection to reduce social risks and they have promoted mass education as a vehicle for equity (Esping-Andersen, 2002).

Inequalities of income and wealth vary across countries, with the Nordic countries, the Netherlands, Austria, the Czech Republic and Luxembourg having the lowest levels of inequality, and Portugal, the United States, Poland, Turkey and Mexico at the other end of the scale. Although living standards have improved in most OECD countries and welfare systems have been expanding, from the mid-1970s to the mid-1990s, income inequalities have tended to increase (Figure 1.1). Only in Australia, Ireland, France and Denmark have inequalities decreased between the mid-1980s and 2000. Elsewhere inequality has risen since the 1980s, although there were some decreases between the mid-1990s and 2000 (OECD, 2005a).

Figure 1.1. **Income inequality varies across OECD[1]**

Gini coefficient of inequality in the distribution of household disposal income[2]

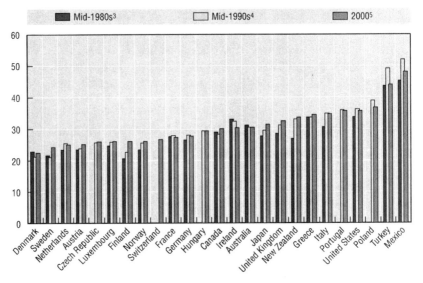

1. Countries ranked in ascending order of income inequalities (from left to right).
2. The Gini coefficient values range between 0 in the case of perfect equality implying that each share of the population gets the same share of income, and 100 in the case of perfect inequality, meaning that all income goes to the share of the population with the highest income.
3. Mid-1980s data refer to the year 1983 in Austria, Belgium, Denmark and Sweden; 1984 in Australia, France, Italy and Mexico; 1985 in Canada, Japan, the Netherlands and the United Kingdom; 1986 in Finland, Luxembourg, New Zealand and Norway; 1987 in Ireland and Turkey, 1988 in Greece; and 1989 in the United States. Data for Germany in the mid-1980s refer to western *Länder* only.
4. Mid-1990s data refer to the year 1995 in all countries except 1993 for Austria; 1994 for Australia, Denmark, France, Germany, Greece, Ireland, Japan, Mexico and Turkey; and 1996 for the Czech Republic and New Zealand.
5. 2000 data refer to the year 2000 in all countries except 1999 for Australia, Austria and Greece; 2001 for Germany, Luxembourg, New Zealand and Switzerland; and 2002 for the Czech Republic, Mexico and Turkey.

Source: OECD (2005a), *Society at a Glance*, OECD, Paris.

The distribution of income depends on earnings, employment and capital income, and on how government redistributes income through taxes and transfers. Governments have continued their focus on social protection, social

Box 1.3. **Recognising equity and inequity**

"Philosophers have been struggling for a long time to clarify what might be meant in social policy by the term 'equity'. Summarizing that discussion, let alone seeking to add to it, is beyond the capacity and fortunately, beyond the scope of this publication. There is general agreement that the aim of public policy cannot and should not be equality in the sense that everyone is the same or achieves the same outcomes – a state that appears to be both impossible and undesirable. Rather, a commitment to equity suggests that differences in outcomes should not be attributable to differences in areas such as wealth, income, power or possessions. The question is then of what state or degree of inequality is acceptable. The answer to this question will always be a contested one, fought out in political arenas of all kinds on a continuing basis. The grounds of this struggle seem to have shifted in the last 30 years towards reducing the gap in outcomes between the top and bottom by helping those at the bottom move up. This may be unsatisfactory as a definition from an analytic perspective but is workable from the standpoint of policy. The argument has been made about quality (Pirsig, 1974) that while we may not be able to define it, we know it when we see it. For equity, it may be that while we cannot define what it is, we know when we are far from it." (Levin, 2003)

cohesion and education as a way to act upon the problems of poverty and income inequality in different countries. Thus, governments play a significant role in accelerating or moderating trends in income distribution and poverty (OECD, 2005b) and education is a key in this strategy, as it is one of the key contributors to productivity and earnings.

In terms of wages, Nickell (2004) has shown that most of the cross-country variation in earning inequality can be assigned to cross-country variation in skill dispersion. The distribution of educational attainment is crucial to explaining the dispersion of earnings and poverty (Schütz and Wössmann, 2006). Providing education and training for all is, therefore, important to increase labour market participation and to reduce social exclusion of particular groups (Brunello and de Paola, 2006).

For education, two questions arise. What role has education played in the past in these changing patterns of inequality, and how can education policy act in the future to limit these inequalities?

1.4. Why equity in education?

This background of income inequality is important, but it is not the only reason for pursuing equity in education. Education has been found to be a determinant of economic growth and individual life chances in terms of both wages and employment opportunities, while the development of what we know as knowledge societies has raised the value of education and skills (Box 1.4). At the same time, globalisation and increased migration are changing the structure of populations in OECD countries and posing equity and social cohesion challenges. Overall, greater equity in educational opportunities can improve the life chances of individuals, support social equity and reduce public costs to society without necessarily damaging efficiency.

Box 1.4. **Equity in the knowledge economy**

"We cannot afford not to be egalitarians in the advanced economies of the 21st century. There are inevitably basic questions of social justice involved. But there is a very good argument that equality of opportunities and life chances is becoming *sine qua non* for efficiency as well. Our human capital constitutes the single most important resource that we must mobilise in order to ensure a dynamic and competitive knowledge economy. We are facing huge demographic imbalances with very small working age cohorts ahead, and to sustain the elderly we must maximise the productivity of the young and immigrants." (Esping-Andersen, 2002)

- *Education enhances life chances of individuals:* Education is a key determinant of both wages and employment opportunities (Booth *et al.*, 2002; Dearden *et al.*, 2000; Ok and Tergeist, 2003) and non-economic outcomes such as good health, longevity, and successful parenting (Dearden *et al.*, 2000; Vernez *et al.*, 1999; Osberg, 1998).

- *Equity in education supports social equity:* Given that education is such a powerful determinant of life chances, equity in education supports equity in life chances. A recent OECD study shows that education is a major contributor to the inheritance of economic advantages across generations and to social stratification, but by the same token is the most accessible policy instrument available to increase intergenerational income mobility (OECD, 2006a). Nickell (2004), for example, shows that trends in the cross-country variation in earnings inequality can be explained by variation in skill dispersion, and the distribution of educational attainment is crucial to explaining the dispersion of earnings and poverty. It follows that if public policy aims to promote social equity, equity in education will be an essential ingredient in the policy mix. Furthermore, education has been seen as a key vehicle to improve the integration of immigrants – through language support and by facilitating the transmission of norms and values that provide the basis for social cohesion.

- *Unequal results in education have heavy costs*: School failures and dropouts are more at risk of benefit dependency, juvenile delinquency and the associated costs to society (Lochner and Moretti, 2004; Schütz and Wössmann, 2006; McMahon 2002). Some modelling exercises suggest that improving the educational attainment of the disadvantaged can pay over the long run, not only through long-term savings in income transfer, public social programmes and public health, but also through the resulting increase in tax revenues and higher disposable income for those involved (Rand, 2003; Statistics Canada and OECD, 2001). Other research has demonstrated that the greater the educational inequality, the lower the levels of social cohesion (Green *et al.*, 2003, Dayton-Johnson, 2001).

- *Public expenditure on education reduces initial income differences*: An OECD study on public expenditure shows that spending on education reduces initial differences in income, mainly because progressive taxation bears more heavily on the better-off and is used to fund education for all, at least in the compulsory phase. Spending on pre-primary and compulsory education significantly narrows income inequalities, as it is the population in the lower tail of income distribution that benefits the most. Expenditure on tertiary education sometimes makes no difference to income inequality, but in many countries it favours the affluent, widening income inequality (OECD, 2006b).

- *Equity in education is an end in itself*: Equity is widely seen as one of the basic necessities of life and the right to education is recognised, for example, in the United Nations Declaration of the Rights of the Child and the constitution of most nations.

- *There is no contradiction between equity and efficiency in education*: Some economists have argued that redistribution of resources to the needy helps equity but damages efficiency, since it involves confiscating some of the returns from hard work and enterprise to assist those worst off. Others have disagreed. A recent World Bank report argues that equity and efficiency are in fact complementary in economic development (World Bank, 2006). Within basic education, the economists' trade-off between equity and efficiency is hard to discern. School failure has large costs not only to those involved, but also to society, because the welfare costs of marginalised persons is large. Thus, reasonably priced and effective cures will benefit both efficiency and equity (Box 1.3). The European Union has called on its member states to support both equity and efficiency in education, as they are mutually reinforcing (Council of the European Union, 2006; Commission of the European Communities, 2006). Some studies suggest that an equitable distribution of skills across populations also has a strong impact on overall economic performance (Coulombe *et al.*, 2004).

References

Barth, E. and C. Lucifora (2006), "Wage Dispersion, Markets and Institutions: The Effect of the Boom in Education on the Wage Structure", *Institute for the Study of Labor (IZA)Discussion Paper*, No. 2181.

Baye, A., M. Demeuse, C. Monseur, C. Goffin (2006), *A Set of Indicators to Measure Equity in 25 European Union Education Systems*, European Commission, University of Liège.

Booth, A. and M. Bryan (2002), "Who Pays for General Training? New Evidence for British Men and Women", *IZA Discussion Paper*, No. 486, April.

Budria, S. and P. Pereira (2005), "Educational Qualifications and Wage Inequality: Evidence for Europe", *IZA Discussion Paper* No. 1763.

Budria, S. and A. Egido (2005), "Education, Over-Education, and Wage Inequality: Evidence for Spain", *Munich Personal RePEc Archive*, Paper No. 93.

Commission of the European Communities (2006), Communication from the Commission to the Council and to the European Parliament, *Efficiency and Equity in European Education and Training Systems*, SEC(2006)1096.

Coulombe, S., S. Marchand and J. Tremblay, (2004), *International Adult Literacy Survey, Literacy Scores, Human Capital and Growth across Fourteen OECD Countries*, Statistics Canada, Ottawa.

Council of the European Union (2006), *Conclusions of the Council and the Representatives of the Governments of the Member States, Meeting within the Council, on Efficiency and Equity in Education and Training*, 15 November 2006.

Dayton-Johnson, J. (2001), *Social Cohesion and Economic Prosperity*, James Lorimer and Co., Toronto.

Dearden, L., H. Reed and J. Van Reenen (2000), "Estimates of the impact of improvements in basic skills on aggregate wages, employment, taxes and benefits", in J. Bynner (ed.), *The Social Benefits of Basic Skills*, DfEE Research Centre on the Wider Benefits of Learning, London.

Esping-Andersen, G. (2002), *Why We Need a New Welfare State*, Oxford University Press, Oxford.

Green, A., J. Preston and R. Sabates (2003), "Education, Equality and Social Cohesion: a Distributional Approach", *Compare*, Vol. 33, No. 4, December, Routledge, pp. 453-470.

Levin, B. (2003), *Approaches to Equity in Policy for Lifelong Learning*, a paper commissioned by the Education and Training Policy Division, OECD, for the Equity in Education Thematic Review, *www.oecd.org/dataoecd/50/16/38692676.pdf*.

Lochner, L. and E. Moretti (2004), "The Effects of Education on Crime: Evidence from Prison Inmates, Arrests and Self-Reports", *American Economic Review* 94 (1), pp. 155-189.

Martins, P. and P. Pereira (2004), "Does Education Reduce Wage Inequality? Quantile Regression Evidence from 16 Countries", *Labour Economics*, Vol. 11 (2004), pp. 355-371.

McMahon, W. (2002), *Education and Development: Measuring the Social Benefits*, Oxford University Press, Oxford.

Nickell, S. (2004), "Poverty and Worklessness in Britain", *Economic Journal*, Vol. 114, Royal Economic Society, Blackwell Publishing, Oxford, pp. C1-C25.

OECD (2003), *The Sources of Economic Growth in OECD Countries*, OECD, Paris.

OECD (2004a), *Equity in Education: Students with Disabilities, Learning Difficulties and Disadvantages*, OECD, Paris.

OECD (2005a), *Society at a Glance*, OECD, Paris.

OECD (2005b), *Extending Opportunities: How Active Social Policy Can Benefit Us All*, OECD, Paris.

OECD (2006a), "Intergenerational Transmission of Disadvantage", Directorate for Employment, Labour and Social Affairs, OECD, Paris.

OECD (2006b), "Publicly Provided Goods and the Distribution of Resources", Directorate for Employment, Labour and Social Affairs, OECD, Paris.

Ok, W. and P. Tergeist (2003), "Improving Workers' Skills: Analytical Evidence and the Role of the Social Partners," *OECD Social Employment and Migration Working Papers* 10, OECD Directorate for Employment, Labour and Social Affairs, Paris.

Osberg, L. (1998), "Economic Policy Variables and Population Health", in *Canada Health Action: Determinants of Health: Settings and Issues*, Vol. 3, MultiMondes, Sainte-Foy, Québec, pp. 579-610.

Pirsig, R. (1974), *Zen and the Art of Motorcycle Maintenance*, Bantam, New York.

Schütz, G. and L. Wössmann (2006), *Efficiency and Equity in European Education and Training Systems*, prepared by the European Expert Network in Economics in Education to accompany the Communication and Staff Working Paper by the European Commission under the same title, *http://ec.europa.eu/education/policies/2010/doc/eenee.pdf*.

Statistics Canada and OECD (2001), *Literacy, Numeracy and Labour Market Outcomes in Canada*, Statistics Canada, Ottawa and OECD, Paris.

Vernez, G., R. Krop and P. Rydell (1999), *Closing the Education Gap: Benefits and Costs*, Rand, Santa Monica.

World Bank (2005), *World Development Report 2006: Equity and Development*, World Bank and Oxford University Press, Washington DC and New York.

ISBN 978-92-64-03259-0
No More Failures: Ten Steps to Equity in Education
© OECD 2007

Chapter 2

A Look at Inequities in Education

This chapter summarises selected quantitative evidence of equity in education and lays the groundwork for the policy chapters that follow. It starts by looking at the historical expansion of education and whether it has helped equity, noting the gains by women and the more disappointing evidence on other fronts. It then examines how inequalities change and develop over the lifecycle, the different phases of education and the position of vulnerable groups including migrants and dropouts. Expanding on the previous chapter, it explores how fairness and inclusion are intertwined, as it is often the disadvantaged who are underperforming, and how inequities may be perpetuated by features of the education system.

Figure 2.1. **Younger people have higher levels of education**

Percentage of the population with upper secondary education, by age group (2005)[1]

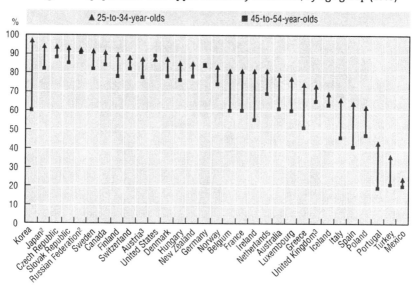

1. Excluding ISCED 3C short programmes.
2. Year of reference 2003.
3. Including some ISCED 3C short programmes.

Source: OECD (2007), Education at a Glance: OECD Indicators 2007, OECD, Paris.

as to enhance equity. In others, expansion may have actually damaged equity. There is a variety of evidence to illustrate these patterns:

● Everywhere, social origin remains important to attainment in basic schooling. On average in OECD countries, students at age 15 from poorer backgrounds (the lowest quartile of socio-economic status) are twice as likely to end up in the lowest quartile for reading and science performance, and three times as likely to end up in the lowest quartile for mathematics performance as they would have been if social background had no effect (OECD, 2001; OECD, 2004b).

● In many OECD countries, tertiary education remains dominated by students from well educated backgrounds. In 1995, young people whose parents had tertiary education were between two and six times more likely to complete tertiary education than those whose parents had less than secondary education. Although in absolute terms, young people from poor backgrounds were much more likely than before to enter tertiary education in 1995, relatively speaking a young person from a more advantaged background remained much more likely to get in (Hiroshi et al., 1995).

Figure 2.2. **Women moving ahead?**

Difference between men and women in number of years spent in formal education, for two different age groups (2004)

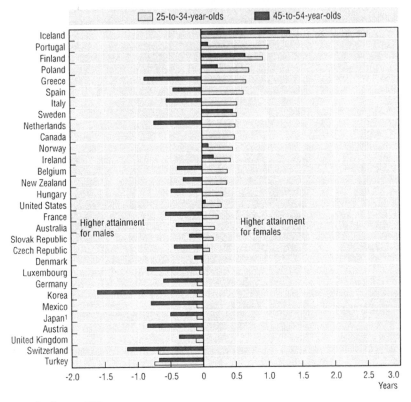

1.   Year of reference 2003.

Source: OECD (2006c), *Education at a Glance: OECD Indicators 2006*, OECD, Paris.

- Educational expansion has a varying impact on social mobility. Nordic countries tend to have higher mobility than others, and in Finland there is evidence that social mobility has increased, perhaps particularly since the introduction of comprehensive schooling (Pekkarinen *et al.*, 2006). Erikson and Jonsson (1996) found that the association between class origin and educational attainment has declined across cohorts in Sweden and Germany, but not in England, and that inequality remains greatest in Germany. Another study suggests that the Nordic countries (especially Norway and Sweden) appear to be among the most open countries, while Germany, France and Italy tend to have a rigid class structure with low mobility. In the United Kingdom, tertiary education appears to have helped middle-class people to pass on their advantages to their children (Blanden *et al.*, 2005). The United States has also been found to be rigid, especially

differences, in this respect the vast majority of countries lie in a fairly narrow band (Shavit and Blossfeld, 1993; Erikson and Jonsson, 1996; OECD, 2001; OECD, 2004b).

Differences between and across schools and performance

PISA also offers one very striking result. Any individual student outcome is correlated not only with that individual's own social background, but also with the social background of other students in the same school. Figure 2.4 shows differences in student results from different schools (between-school variance) and from the same school (within-school variance). While all countries show large within-school variance, in most countries between-school variance is also wide and explained in significant part by the social mix of students in different schools.

In some countries, there is little association between individual performance and the schools children attend. This includes the Nordic countries, Poland, the United Kingdom, the United States, Canada, Ireland, New Zealand, Australia, Spain and Mexico. On the other side, in countries like Germany, Austria, Italy, Japan and Hungary, there are large differences between schools, much of it linked to the socio-economic background of schools and students.

Adults: to those that hath shall be given

Adults who have more initial education tend to participate more in later education. People leave formal education with unequal attainment and these inequalities then widen over time as better educated adults seek and obtain more subsequent training (Figure 2.5), as well as undertaking work using and developing higher level skills (OECD, 2005d). The implication is twofold. First, initial education needs to ensure that everyone gains sufficient basic skills, and sufficient engagement with education and the learning process to be able to upgrade those skills later. Second, well targeted second chance programmes need to concentrate their efforts on those with the lowest levels of qualifications. Figure 2.5 shows that some countries are much more successful at this than others. Participation of low skilled adults in learning is important not only for their own sake but also for their children, as better-educated parents can better support the learning of their children.

Overall, on fairness, socio-economic status remains important to attainment in basic schooling everywhere (Marks et al., 2006). Students from poorer backgrounds (the lowest quartile of socio-economic status) were on average twice as likely as the average OECD student to end up in the lowest quartile for reading and science performance at age 15, and three times as likely to end up in the lowest quartile for math performance (OECD, 2001;

Figure 2.4. **Attainment and the social mix in schools**

Variance (spread) in student performance in mathematics between schools
and within schools expressed as a percentage of the average variance[1]
in student performance in OECD countries (100) and the impact of socio-economic
status of students and schools on the variance in student performance[2] (2003)

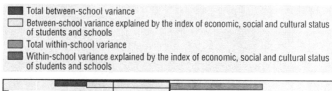

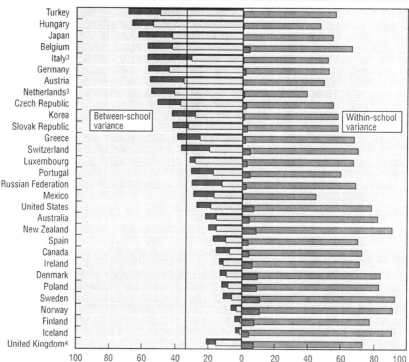

1. Average variance in student performance (100) is composed of the average variance between schools (33.6, attributable to the difference in student results attained by students in different schools) and the average variance within schools (67, attributable to the range of student results within schools).
2. Variance in student performance, explained by the index of economic, social and cultural status of students and schools, indicates how much of the variance is attributable to the SES of students, either between or within schools.
3. For example, between-school variance is similar in Italy and the Netherlands, but the amount of this variance that is explained by the socio-economic background of the students is greater in the Netherlands than in Italy.
4. Response rate too low to ensure comparability.

Source: OECD (2004b), *Learning for Tomorrow's World: First Results from PISA 2003*, OECD, Paris.

OECD, 2004b). At the two extremes, someone from the lowest quartile of socio-economic status in Switzerland is 2.7 times more likely to end up in the lowest quartile for reading, while in Finland the comparable figure is 1.5.

Figure 2.5. **The well-qualified make most use of adult education**

Relative chances of adults with tertiary education participating in adult learning compared to those with only primary education (2003)

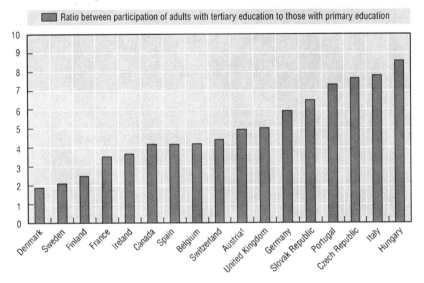

1. For example, in Austria a university graduate is five times more likely to participate in adult learning than an adult with primary education.

Source: European Labour Force Survey, 2003.

Improvements by the worst performing countries up to an internationally determined benchmark would therefore yield improvements in the life chances of those from low socio-economic backgrounds. In Switzerland, for example, the relevant figure might be reduced from 2.7 to the OECD average of 2.0.

2.3. Equity as inclusion

Transition from one stage to another

Inclusion implies that all have the minimum skills necessary to function in today's society. Universal completion of compulsory (lower) secondary education is key to this. High rates of transition into and completion of upper secondary school would also imply the provision of the higher level skills required in modern economies. For that reason, universal upper secondary education has become a policy target in some countries. Figure 2.6 shows that at the end of compulsory education and in subsequent stages, a diminishing proportion of the cohort "survives" successive transitions to upper secondary and tertiary education. While there is a set of countries where almost 100% of adults have completed secondary education, this is not true for other countries and transitions from one level to the next show declining rates of

Figure 2.6. **How many continue and how many drop out at different levels of education?**[1]

Percentage of population 25-to-34 years old at different levels of educational attainment (2004)[2]

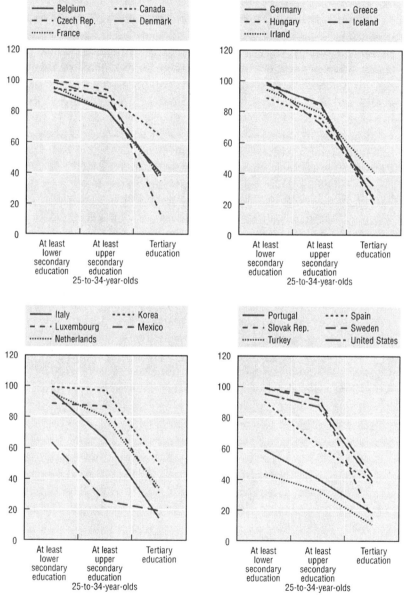

1. It is not possible to show in the figure whether some adults may be going through second chance systems to finalise their education.
2. For Norwegian data, see the Statistics Norway website at *www.ssb.no/English*.
Source: OECD Education Database.

participation. But these transition pictures do not show which groups have a higher propensity to continue at the two key transition points (from lower secondary into upper secondary and from upper secondary into tertiary) and the impact of socio-economic background on these transitions.

Differences in attainment first emerge in children of preschool age, reflecting both personal characteristics and environmental influences. Different mechanisms can then widen or narrow these differences over time. Under some circumstances school systems may reinforce initial inequalities (through lowered expectations, less demanding tracks, or simply losing connection with those who start to fall behind). Alternatively school systems can overcome initial inequalities by helping those who fall behind. But in practice initial differences often widen over time. Farkas (2003) estimated that initial differences may be roughly doubled by the end of the twelfth grade in the United States (see also Shavit and Blossfeld, 1993; Grubb, 2006). Heckman (2000) argues that education is a dynamic process, such that initial learning including both cognitive skills and learning how to learn are preconditions for future learning. The implication is that it is much easier to get a student on a good educational trajectory at the outset than to rectify weaknesses at a later stage.

Participation in early childhood education and care (ECEC)

Enrolment of young children (3-to-6-year-olds) in early childhood education and care is increasingly becoming the norm (Figure 2.7), and some countries offer all children at least three years of free publicly funded provision or access as a statutory right from the age of three (OECD, 2006d). Participation increases sharply with age over the 3-to-6 age span (see Figure 2.7). These raw figures for participation require cautious interpretation: ECEC is highly variable in terms of hours per week, and quality is also sometimes uncertain.

Figure 2.7 also shows that in some countries participation of 3-year-olds in any form of ECEC is weak. In the many countries where early childhood education and care is not free, participation in ECEC is closely related to family income (Chiswick and DebBurnam, 2004; Bainbridge et al., 2005) and disadvantaged children frequently participate less in ECEC, despite evidence that they benefit most (Leseman, 2002; Machin, 2006; OECD, 2006d). We discuss policy measures to increase participation in early childhood education and care in Chapter 5.

Basic skills for all in compulsory education

Many children fail to acquire basic skills at school. On average across the OECD, nearly 22% of 15-year-olds score at and below PISA Level 1 in reading, and 25% score at and below PISA Level 1 in mathematics (OECD 2004b, Tables 2.5a and 6.1). Boys and those who speak a different language at home have

Figure 2.7. **Getting a good start in life**

Participation in ECEC (ISCED 0 and 1), by age (2004)

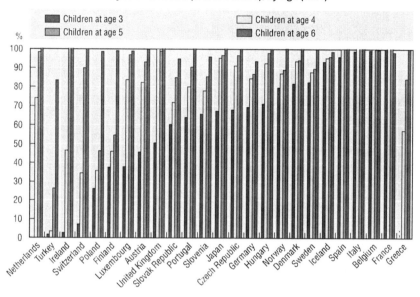

Source: Eurostat.

particular problems with reading skills (OECD 2004b, Tables 6.3 and 4.2g). The impact on those involved is very large, because literacy provides an essential tool for working and living and because it is an essential foundation for nearly all higher level skills. But some countries are extremely effective at minimising failure. Only 6% of Finnish, 7% of Korean and 10% of Canadian 15-year-olds are at and below Level 1 in reading. Only 7% of students in Finland, and 10% in Korea and Canada were at or below Level 1 in mathematics. But in five countries – Greece, Italy, Mexico, Portugal and Turkey – more than 30% of students are at and below Level 1 in mathematics (OECD 2004b, Table 2.5a).

Dropping out

In many OECD countries, upper secondary attainment is considered the educational minimum necessary to participate fully in the labour market and in social life. Those without this level of education are particularly at risk of marginalisation. Figure 2.9 shows that in at least 17 OECD countries, one in ten 20-to-24-year-olds have not completed upper secondary education and were outside of the education system. In some of these countries, including Sweden and the United States, a good proportion of dropouts "drop back in", as there are strong adult learning systems that allow for later completion.

Figure 2.8. **How many students struggle with reading?**[1]

Percentage of students below and at Level 1 of proficiency in the OECD PISA reading scale[2] (2003)

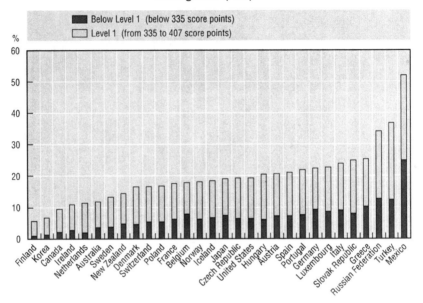

1. Countries are ranked in descending order of percentage of 15-year-olds in Levels 2, 3, 4, 5 and 6.
2. The PISA scale has six levels of proficiency. Level 2 represents the baseline at which students begin having skills that allow them to use reading actively. Level 1 and below imply insufficient reading skills to function in today's societies.

Source: OECD (2004b), *Learning for Tomorrow's World: First Results from PISA 2003*, OECD, Paris.

Thus, on *inclusion*, there are large differences between countries. Enrolment rates in early childhood education and care vary across countries but are reaching high levels at age five. In terms of skills of 15-year-olds, there are large differences in achievement. There are also still too many students who drop out before the end of upper secondary school without the skills necessary to function successfully in society.

2.4. The two dimensions of equity overlap

Looking at the performance of an immigrant group can also provide a picture of how the two dimensions of equity – fairness and inclusion – work together and can be two sides of the same coin. Fairness means that immigrant or socio-economic status should be no barrier. Inclusion means that all those with poor performance need to be assisted, including immigrants.

Immigrants, particularly those who speak a different language than that of the host country, tend to have worse school results. In most countries, first-

Figure 2.9. **How many leave education before the end of upper secondary school?**

Percentage of women and men without upper secondary education and not in education (2002)[1]

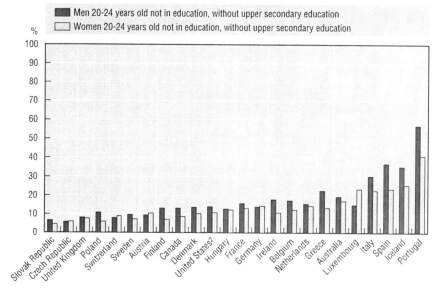

1. According to Norwegian sources, numbers for dropout rates in Norway are approximately 26% for men and 18% for women (see the Statistics Norway website: *www.ssb.no/English*).
2. Year of reference 2001.

Source: OECD (2005e), *From Education to Work: A Difficult Transition for Young Adults with Low Levels of Education*, OECD, Paris.

generation and (to a lesser extent) second-generation immigrant students are out-performed by native students (see Figure 2.10). This suggests some (understandable) disadvantage of newness. The equity issue is whether immigrants are treated fairly, such that their background (after accounting for a "newness effect") does not become an obstacle to achievement.

Among immigrant students, those who speak different languages at home and school do worse at school (their PISA score in mathematics is about 40 points lower). While factors such as socio-economic status, knowledge of the language of instruction and age at migration explain a great deal there remains an unexplained residual of immigrant underachievement in some countries. In Sweden, an important part of the difference between mathematics achievement of first-generation students and that of native students cannot be explained by immigrant background characteristics. In Germany, Denmark and Belgium (Flanders), a substantial part of second-generation immigrant underperformance remains unexplained by social background factors (OECD, 2006e, Table 3.5).

Figure 2.10. **Weaker performance by immigrant students (2003)**

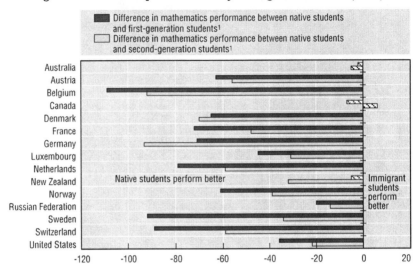

1. Striped bars indicate differences that are not statistically significant.
Source: OECD (2006e), *Where Immigrant Students Succeed: A Comparative Review of Performance and Engagement in PISA 2003*, OECD, Paris.

Immigrant background is also associated with performance variation between schools, particularly in highly tracked education systems, perhaps because immigrant students tend to be channelled to schools with lower performance expectations. In many countries, immigrant students are clustered in certain schools in poor districts. On average, of the OECD countries included in a recent survey (OECD, 2006e, Tables 3.7a and 3.7b), nearly one in three immigrant students (first- and second-generation) attend a school where more than half of the students are also from an immigrant background (OECD, 2006e).

2.5. Policy implications

As explained earlier, equity in education can be considered as having two dimensions: fairness implies that personal and social circumstances should be a minimal obstacle to educational success and inclusion implies a basic minimum standard of education for all.

On *fairness* there are improvements to be made across OECD countries. Throughout successive stages of the education system, those from poor and disadvantaged backgrounds perform less well and participate less often. The effect on final life chances is a cumulative one. Socio-economic background, including parents' educational attainment levels and income, racial or immigrant background and other individual factors all influence educational outcomes.

On *inclusion*, ensuring that all have a minimum level of skills, there are large differences between countries. Consider for example the group of people who are unable to show basic functional reading skills (at or below Level 1 in the PISA score). Large gains could be realised if countries with weak performance were able to raise their performance levels and ensure that a large proportion of children have minimum skills to finish school. Reducing dropout rates would also diminish the proportion of young people who do not reach a minimum level of education.

But there are other factors which also strongly impact on the existence of inequities across countries. These include the structure of the education system and the opportunities it provides, from early childhood education through different pathways in secondary education all the way to adult education. Other factors include the ways in which teaching is organised and delivered in classes, the human and financial resources available in schools and system-level factors such as curricular differences and organisational policies and practices. These issues are covered in the chapters that follow.

Both aspects of equity covered here can be amenable to policy. Within a general framework of policies to promote and commit to success of all students, some strategies may need to focus on compensating for students' low socio-economic background, while others may focus on analysing and modifying education system mechanisms that generate and perpetuate inequalities and discrimination.

The following chapters will analyse different strategies to promote greater equity in education and propose a set of complementary approaches which can be useful to attain both higher performance and reduce the impact of socio-economic background. This set of policy levers (corresponding to Chapters 3, 4 and 5) has been defined to provide a clear framework to better target and deliver equity in education:

- *Design*: Conducive structures and pathways through the education system.
- *Practices*: Inclusive in-school and out-of-school practices.
- *Resourcing*: Equity priorities, resources and targets.

The final chapter, which looks at the special case of migrants and minorities, also contains policy recommendations for practices.

References

Bainbridge, J., M. Meyers, S. Tanaka and J. Waldfogel (2005), "Who Gets an Early Education? Family Income and Enrolment of Three- to Five-Year-Olds from 1968 to 2000", *Social Science Quarterly*, Vol. 86, No. 3, September 2005, Southwestern Social Science Association.

Blanden, J., P. Gregg and S. Machin (2005), *Intergenerational Mobility in Europe and North America*, Centre for Economic Performance, London.

Breen, R. and R. Luijkx (2004), "Social Mobility in Europe between 1970 and 2000" in R. Breen (ed.), *Social Mobility in Europe*, Oxford University Press, Oxford, pp. 37-75.

Chiswick, B. and N. DebBurnam (2004), "Pre-School Enrollment: An Analysis by Immigrant Generation", *Centre for Research and Analysis of Migration Discussion Paper*, No. 04/04.

Erikson, R. and J. Jonsson (eds.) (1996), *Can Education be Equalized: The Swedish Case in Comparative Perspective*, Westview Press, Boulder, Colorado.

Farkas, G. (2003), "Racial Disparities and Discrimination in Education: What Do We know, How Do We Know It, and What Do We Need to Know?", *Teachers College Record* 105(6).

Heckman, J. (2000), "Policies to Foster Human Capital", *Research in Economics*, Vol. 54, No. 1, pp. 3-56.

Hiroshi, I., W. Muller and J. Ridges (1995), "Class Origin, Class Destination, and Education: A Cross-National Study of Ten Industrial Nations", *American Journal of Sociology*, 101(1), pp. 145-93.

Leseman, P. (2002), *Early Childhood and Care for Children from Low-Income or Minority Backgrounds*, Discussion Paper at the OECD Oslo Workshop, 6-7 June 2002, OECD, Paris.

Machin, S. (2006), "Social Disadvantage and Education Experiences", *OECD Social, Employment and Migration Working Papers*, No. 32, Directorate for Employment, Labour and Social Affairs, OECD, Paris.

Marks, G., J. Cresswell and J. Ainley (2006), "Explaining Socioeconomic Inequalities in Student Achievement: The Role of Home and School Factors, "*Educational Research and Evaluation*, Vol. 12, No. 2, April, pp. 105-128.

OECD (2001), *Knowledge and Skills for Life: First Results from PISA 2000*, OECD, Paris.

OECD (2004b), *Learning for Tomorrow's World: First Results from PISA 2003*, OECD, Paris.

OECD (2005a), *Society at a Glance*, OECD, Paris.

OECD (2005b), *Extending Opportunities: How Active Social Policy Can Benefit Us All*, OECD, Paris.

OECD (2005c), *Education at a Glance: OECD Indicators 2005*, OECD, Paris.

OECD (2005d), *Promoting Adult Learning*, OECD, Paris.

OECD (2005e), *From Education to Work: A Difficult Transition for Young Adults with Low Levels of Education*, OECD, Paris.

OECD (2006b), "Publicly Provided Goods and the Distribution of Resources", Directorate for Employment, Labour and Social Affairs, OECD, Paris.

OECD (2006c), *Education at a Glance: OECD Indicators 2006*, OECD, Paris.

OECD (2006d), *Starting Strong II: Early Childhood Education and Care*, OECD, Paris.

OECD (2006e), *Where Immigrant Students Succeed: A Comparative Review of Performance and Engagement in PISA 2003*, OECD, Paris.

OECD (2007c), *Education at a Glance: OECD Indicators 2007*, OECD, Paris.

Pekkarinen, T., S. Pekkala and R. Uusitalo (2006), "Education Policy and Intergenerational Income Mobility: Evidence from the Finnish Comprehensive School Reform", *IZA Discussion Paper*, No. 2204.

Shavit and Blossfeld (1993), *Persistent Inequality: Changing Educational Attainment in Thirteen Countries*, Westview Press, Boulder, Colorado.

ISBN 978-92-64-03259-0
No More Failures: Ten Steps to Equity in Education
© OECD 2007

Chapter 3

Structures and Pathways

This chapter looks at the design of education systems – how they are put together and the routes through them – to analyse their impact on equity. It examines selection and choice in basic education, the different pathways in secondary and post-secondary education and explores evidence on how conducive these features may be to equity. Wherever these processes direct students to separate pathways (a process known as differentiation) and students in the separated pathways have different experiences, initial inequalities may be lessened or increased. The chapter argues that selection and choice create risks for equity which have to be managed, for example by using random lotteries rather than academic selection to choose successful applicants for schools in high demand. In addition, attractive secondary education structures and pathways without dead ends contribute to equity, as do effective systems of second chance education for those who did not finish when young.

Navigating a pathway through an education system is a challenge for anyone. Often it may seem like an obstacle course or a maze with few signposts and many dead ends. Some students get better guidance than others, from parents or other adults who can point the way and help avoid traps and pitfalls. Others have to find their own way. Some have to pay to pass by favoured routes while those who cannot pay follow slower and congested routes. It is hardly surprising that some give up the struggle, fall by the wayside or end up somewhere they never expected or wanted to be. This chapter looks at why education systems often appear to have this character, and what can be done to improve them.

3.1. Differentiation in schooling structures and the risks to equity

As discussed in Chapter 2, initial inequalities often increase with age and the education system can either reinforce or help to overcome that tendency. This section looks at how *academic selection* and *school choice* can help to increase or reduce these initial differences. As a convention we refer to decisions made by the education system as *selection* of students and decisions made by students (and sometimes their parents) as *choice*.

Differentiation, spread throughout the education system, can have an additive effect. The student composition of any given classroom can depend on a number of preceding filters. For example, a highly selective educational system, with selective secondary schools, streaming within schools and separate schools for most students with special needs, may yield, through a process of successive distillation, classrooms which are extremely homogeneous in terms of attainment.

Any given pathway (for example an academic track in secondary school) affects learning in two ways. First, the teaching environment may be distinctive, because of the curriculum, teacher quality, pedagogic approach or teaching resources. Second, students may be affected by the students alongside them – the peer-group effect. PISA evidence shows that the social composition of the school is strongly related to individual outcomes, independently of the social background of the individual student (see OECD, 2004d, Figure 4.11). Previous research has reached the same conclusion. Hanushek *et al.* (2001), for example, showed that in Texas schools, a 0.1 standard deviation increase in peer average achievement leads to a roughly 0.02 standard deviation increase in achievement of the student.

NO MORE FAILURES: TEN STEPS TO EQUITY IN EDUCATION – ISBN 978-92-64-03259-0 – © OECD 2

Social differentiation among schools can be due to selection in the education system as well as the tendency for different social groups to live in different areas. Figure 3.1 presents an index of separation showing the levels of social sorting across schools in OECD countries. As can be seen, there is a wide variation in these practices, with the Nordic countries on one hand showing quite similar schools in terms of social composition, while countries such as Austria, Belgium, Germany, Hungary, Mexico, the Slovak Republic and Turkey have a high degree of social differentiation across their schools.

Figure 3.1. **Social sorting between schools**

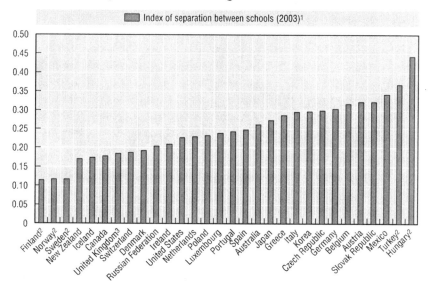

1. The index of separation shows the extent to which a country has sorted children (15-year-olds) from different socio-economic backgrounds into different schools, with zero representing a country in which all schools have a similar social composition. The index is developed with the ESCS, the PISA index of economic, social and cultural status. See Annex A1 in OECD (2004b), *Learning for Tomorrow's World: First Results from PISA 2003*, Paris.
2. For example, in Finland, Norway and Sweden, all schools have a similar social distribution; in Hungary and Turkey, individual schools have very different social composition.
3. Response rate too low to ensure comparability.

Source: OECD (2004b), *Learning for Tomorrow's World: First Results from PISA 2003*, OECD, Paris.

There are at least three reasons for thinking that social separation between schools may be a problem. First, it can certainly be argued that a sense of common culture and citizenship is most readily developed if children from different backgrounds are educated together. Second, systems with a high level of school separation have worse results overall in maths and reading (Annex 3.1). As already mentioned, the social composition of a school is strongly associated with school outcomes. A full explanation of these outcomes would be complex, no doubt because the reasons for separation of schools are themselves quite diverse. Third, the concentration of disadvantaged children in certain schools undoubtedly increases the challenge of working in those schools. Depending on how teachers' careers are managed and on financial incentives, more able teachers often choose to avoid teaching in those schools, adding to the obstacles facing disadvantaged children. Chapter 5 examines evidence for this phenomenon.

Academic selection: the risks to equity

Often, students are sorted into different pathways according to their academic performance. This may involve a paper and pencil test, an informal assessment of attainment or a formal qualification. Academic selection is very common in entry to upper secondary education, for example in France for entry to *lycées* or in Finland for determining who enters the academic rather than vocational track. In almost all countries, academic selection determines entry to institutions at tertiary level, particularly to elite institutions. Figure 3.2 shows the extent of reported academic selection in lower and upper secondary schools. This may cover selection into individual schools as well as selection into, for example, an academic rather than a vocational track.

Figure 3.2. **Where attainment determines the school attended**

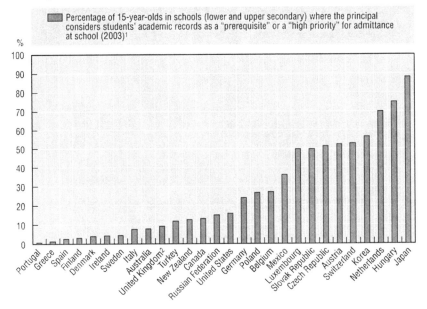

1. This category – "admittance by attainment" – does not apply to Norway and Iceland.
2. Response rate too low to ensure comparability.
Source: OECD (2004b), *Learning for Tomorrow's World: First Results from PISA 2003*, OECD, Paris.

Sometimes, as in Hungary, popular secondary schools may organise an entrance exam. In other countries, in Norway for example, for lower secondary schools, there is virtually no selection on the grounds of academic record (Mortimore *et al.*, 2005). But all education systems use academic selection at some stage. The main differences internationally are between education systems which use academic selection at early stages and those which leave it until upper secondary or tertiary level. Eight out of ten countries with the highest index of separation start selection before the age of 15; among countries with the lowest index of separation, only one starts selection before the age of 15 (see OECD 2004c, Figure 5.20a).

Academic selection can have positive features. It may help both stronger and weaker performers by adapting learning environments to the needs of each group, permitting each group to learn at its own pace, providing a reward in the form of entrance to a desired institution on a track that encourages attainment. Conversely, it is often argued that academic selection hinders the learning of those who are not selected for the following reasons:

- *Poor quality education:* High quality and high status programmes and institutions are naturally in high demand. When academic selection is used to choose entrants, those with initially weaker attainment can end up with lower quality education.

- *Lack of benefit from peer-group effects:* Weaker performers are not able to benefit from the expectations and aspirations of stronger performers and thus improve their own performance.

- *Stigma:* Sorting based on attainment tends to stigmatise those who do not meet the attainment standard, labelling them as poor performers and reducing their prospects in future education or in the labour market.

- *Unreliable sorting:* Prior attainment levels, particularly at young ages, are a weak guide to future potential (Brunello *et al.*, 2005).

Where these factors are dominant, those not selected will lose out. Any initial gap in performance would then widen, increasing the inequality of educational outcomes. Since many initial differences in performance are attributable to social background, the differential impact of social background on life chances would also be increased. Academic selection might therefore increase both inequality of outcomes and the impact of socio-economic status on outcomes. Some empirical analysis based on PISA data provides evidence on the associations between academic selection and potential impact on equity:

- PISA data shows no statistically significant correlation between academic selection and either average country results or the spread of results. However, countries with more academic selection also showed more students with high mathematics scores (Level 6 and above) and science scores (more than 600 points) – but not more with strong reading skills (see Annex 3.2.1). There was no association with the proportion of low-level performers.

● On the other hand, PISA evidence shows that countries using more academic selection tend also to show a stronger effect of social background on individual performance (see Annex 3.2.2).

● Academic selection by schools is also often associated with more social separation between schools (see Annex 3.2.3), but in fact the relationship is strongly mediated by school choice (see Annex 3.2.4). Bjorklund et al. (2004) looked at the effect of a Swedish school reform which allowed independent schools in Stockholm to select by ability. Following the reform, segregation across schools (in respect of factors like immigrant status, and parental income) increased markedly, suggesting that in this case the association between selection and segregation was causal. Similar results are reported in England by Fitz et al. (2001).

Sometimes, given school choice, academic selection may be used by over-subscribed schools to select students. Individual schools have incentives to use academic selection, since children who already have good results may be easier to teach and have fewer disadvantages of social background to affect their performance and behaviour at school. Table 3.1 shows that a number of OECD countries allow over-subscribed schools to use academic selection to choose students but many other criteria are also used to select students. In Spain, for example, selection reflects factors such as family income, enrolment of siblings, as well as proximity of home to school.

One potential solution is to require oversubscribed schools to use a lottery to select successful applicants. Here are two examples:

● In Minato City, Tokyo, Japan, successful applicants to elementary and lower secondary schools from outside the district are selected by lottery.

● In Milwaukee, United States, which has an extensive system of school choice, a lottery is used alongside criteria like local residence and having a sibling at the school to choose successful applicants.

Alternatively, as discussed in Chapter 5, if school funding is weighted according to the social circumstances of the school population, popular schools may be offered a financial incentive to preserve an even social mix in the school.

In summary, the evidence points to the fact that early academic selection poses risks to equity, especially in the context of school choice (discussed below). School popularity may reflect quality teaching or strong peer group support for learning or both. The combined effect will be to accelerate the learning of the stronger performers and could create a gap in overall outcomes.

Table 3.1. **Selection and school choice practices**

Country	Do parents have free school choice?	Financial instruments and fees	Selection at school level
Belgium (Flanders)	• Parents may request a school of their preference for their children.	• Grant-aid from the state. • No fees. • In secondary schools, parents may contribute towards the costs of certain school activities and teaching aids.	• First-come first-served basis.
Finland	• Admission primarily according to residence in catchment area but exceptions possible.	• Private schools are financed by the state. • No fees.	• Criteria determined by the Ministry of Education.
France	• Admission primarily according to residence in catchment area but exceptions possible.	• Private schools receive public funding covering part of expenses.	• At upper secondary level: opinion of the class council, family opinion, residence in catchment area.
Hungary	• Admission primarily according to residence in catchment area but exceptions possible.	• *Per capita* state grant for each student (about 60% to 80%), the reminder covered by the maintainer of school. • Church schools receive 100% *per* student *capita* grant funding.	• When demand exceeds supply, selection by ability is possible.
Norway	• At primary and lower secondary level, admission according to residential area. • At upper secondary level school choice within the closest municipalities.	• Private schools usually receive 85% of total expenses.	• No admission requirement in basic school. • At upper secondary level: applicant's grades and the county's course provision. • More than 90% of students are admitted to courses of their first choice.
Slovenia	• Admission primarily according to residence in catchment area but exceptions possible.	• Private preschool institutions and schools receive 85% of funds provided by the state or by the municipality.	• When demand exceeds supply, selection by ability is possible.
Spain	• Parents may request a school of their preference for their children.	• Private schools (*centros concertados*) receive grants from National Budget. • No fees.	• Annual family income, proximity of the parents' home, prior enrolment of other siblings in the school, size of the family, handicap and previous attendance of children in non-compulsory preschool of the same institution.

Table 3.1. **Selection and school choice practices** (cont.)

Country	Do parents have free school choice?	Financial instruments and fees	Selection at school level
Sweden	• Parents may request a school of their preference for their children.	• Private schools and public schools receive government funding. • No fees.	• If demand exceeds supply selection to public school is based on residence. • Private schools accept students on a first-come first-served basis. • In big cities upper secondary schools can admit students on the basis of their attainment.

Source: School European Journal of Education Research, Development and Policies, "Attitudes, Choice and Participation – Dimensions of the Demand for Schooling" (2006), Vol. 41, No. 1; OECD (2006f), Public Spending Efficiency: Questionnaire on the Pre-Primary, Primary and Lower Secondary Education Sector, OECD/ECO, unpublished; and reports prepared for the Equity in Education Thematic Review (available at www.oecd.org/edu/equity/equityineducation).

School choice

Choosing an institution at which to study is usual in tertiary education and relatively common in upper secondary education. But it is less common and more controversial in basic schooling. In recent years, some countries have increased the extent of choice, particularly in secondary education. This is partly because the demand for choice from parents appears to be increasing and partly because choice is sometimes being promoted by governments as a policy tool to stimulate better performance. For these reasons "school choice" is prominent in public debate and academic research, although the meaning of the expression is often unclear.

Choice, taken literally, might mean the right of parents to decide on which school their child will attend. Such a right might be popular, but in practice it rarely exists, since school places are limited. In fact, regimes described as involving school choice cover many arrangements in which parental preferences have an influence over the schools attended by their children. The outcomes depend not only on the demand for school choice, but also on supply factors – how schools respond to expressed demand and what selection criteria they use when there are more applicants than places. Table 3.1 provides a summary of policy and practice on school choice in countries participating in the Thematic Review on Equity in Education.

School choice arrangements are often defended on the grounds of efficiency, the argument being that a market, or quasi-market, in schooling will push individual schools to improve quality and contain costs (e.g. Hoxby, 2002). We will not assess this argument here, although we note that in international comparisons using PISA, the extent of school choice is not associated with either average mathematics results or their spread. Instead we look at some of the main potential risks for equity presented by school choice.

Informed Demand

In general, informed demand reflects the education level of parents. There is abundant evidence that the informed engagement of parents is helpful to the attainment of the child (Bobbitt and Horn, 2000). This means that those with weaker parental support will be at a disadvantage, whether the issue is supporting homework, or advising on choice of subject of study, or choice of school. Methods for overcoming the inequities arising from home background are discussed in Chapter 4. But risks remain when complex decisions need to be taken, so that the "winners" are the students with the best-educated parents. One particular risk is that well-informed parents may choose schools where the school mix is more affluent. From the point of view of these parents, this may be desirable given that peer group effects may benefit their child but it increases inequities between schools.

Costs

Even when there are no fees, there may be other costs, such as textbooks, uniforms, transportation to school or other expectations of voluntary financial contributions. In the Russian Federation for example, informal costs – such as for textbooks and extra lessons – have a significant effect on the choice of school (Ministry of Education, Russian Federation, 2005).

In the traditional neighbourhood school model, well-off parents can choose schools for their children by buying or renting accommodation in the relevant catchment area. Often desirable schools tend to be in better off areas with higher property prices and rents. Sometimes, the defined catchment areas of good schools increase the price of accommodation in those areas (Gibbons and Machin, 2001). The perverse effect is that although schooling is provided free, schooling perceived to be of good quality has an implicit price in the housing market.

Parents may choose private schools, either fully independent schools which charge fees and receive no government funding or those which, although privately managed, receive government subsidies and charge no fees or very low fees. Dronkers and Robert (2003) found that while the subsidised sector is more effective than the government sector (mainly because of a better school climate), the fully private sector is less effective, after taking account of peer-group effects of the student population. These results may appear surprising. Private schools are often more costly than state schools. In addition, it could be supposed that market pressures in the private sector would encourage efficiencies. Why do they not do so? One answer is that local monopolies may be involved. Fee-paying private schools only cater to the wealthier sections of society and, given travelling distances, there may be limited local competition. Under these circumstances, a private school may find it profitable to provide a learning environment which is of similar quality to local state schools. Parents will still choose to send their children to the private school because its social composition may yield a better learning environment overall than public schools – particularly once the school is established and has skimmed off the more socially advantaged students in local schools.

The effects of school choice on the social mix of schools

In practice, countries with more school choice also tend to have school systems which are more socially separated (see Figure 3.3). (In this analysis, school choice was measured through an inverse PISA proxy – the extent to which place of residence determines school admission.) When the joint effect of school choice and academic selection was examined, school choice emerged as the prime driver of separation, while academic selection became statistically insignificant (see Annex 3.2.2). Conceivably, more socially

Figure 3.3. **Does school choice increase social differences between schools? (2003)**

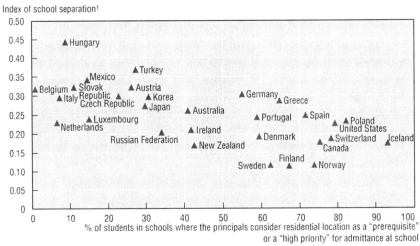

1. The index of separation shows the extent to which a country has sorted children (15-year-olds) from different socio-economic backgrounds into different schools, with zero representing a country in which all schools have a similar social composition. ile index is developed with the ESCS, the PISA index of economic, social and cultural status. See Annex A1 in OECD (2004b), *Learning for Tomorrow's World: First Results from PISA 2003*, OECD, Paris.

Source: OECD (2004b), *Learning for Tomorrow's World: First Results from PISA 2003*, OECD, Paris.

separated schools may increase the demand for school choice (as well as being the result of school choice) with middle-class parents seeking to escape the perceived risks of schools with many children from deprived backgrounds. Although the causal relationships are uncertain, the risks to equity of school choice – particularly through social polarization of schools – are sufficiently salient to require careful management, avoiding academic selection as much as possible and using measures such as lotteries in order to ensure a social balance in school intake.

In Spain, concern over the potential weakening of comprehensive schooling through segregation based on unequal real choice led at least the regional government of Catalunya to develop a policy of co-ordinated, area-based provision, centred on educational zones in Barcelona (Teese et al., 2005). The regional and local governments have jointly formed an Education Consortium (approved in 2002, but only recently brought into operation) to develop a strong education network of schools taking into consideration social cohesion principles.

3.2. Early tracking and comprehensive schooling

Many education systems contain mechanisms for dividing students into separate types of education, with different curricula, different qualifications at the end of the programme and different expectations of transition to further education or work, representing different *tracks*. Commonly, more academic tracks offer readier access to tertiary education, and vocational tracks provide training for particular jobs or trades in the labour market (although these may also provide options for continued education). The division into separate tracks usually takes place at different levels during secondary education. In Hungary for example, children aged around 12 (about 6% in 2005/06) can apply for admittance to different tracks. Other students move at the age of 14 to one of three different tracks: an academic school potentially leading to tertiary education, a vocational school providing vocational qualifications and giving access to tertiary education, or a short programme of vocational training in another type of school leading to early departure from school and entry into the labour market. In other countries, for example in Finland, Norway and Sweden, the division between academic and vocational tracks occurs at upper secondary level.

Many OECD countries have introduced comprehensive education up to about the age of 15, typically abolishing tracked lower secondary education in the process. The Nordic countries were among the first to make the change more than a generation ago, while Spain introduced the reform as recently as the early 1990s by adding two more years of comprehensive schooling. A number of countries in Central Europe retain systems which divide children between vocational and more academic tracks in early adolescence. In some countries, even though there is no nationwide or regional system of tracking, informal tracking may emerge locally, through selection into different schools or because different streams within schools offer different curricula. This characterises the position, for example, in some parts of the United States. Academic selection is normally important in determining which track students enter. In many countries, those with higher attainment typically enter academic tracks (although Sweden and Norway represent an important exception, in that they have no threshold of academic attainment required for entry into general upper secondary education). To some extent, all the potential risks to equity associated with academic selection also apply to tracked systems. But choice is also a factor, and students aiming for a particular occupation for which vocational education is important may opt for that track even when their school results would have permitted them to follow an academic track.

Effects of early tracking on equity and quality

Countries with early tracking performed less well on average in PISA 2000 than countries with more comprehensive education systems (OECD, 2005e). In PISA 2003, neither the number of distinct tracks nor the age at first selection were found to have a statistically significant relationship with either average mathematics performance or the spread of performance (the standard deviation, see OECD, 2004d, Figure 5.20b, p. 263). However the effect of social background on performance – an indicator of inequity – was clearly stronger in countries with earlier ages of selection and a larger number of separate tracks. Hanushek and Wössmann (2005) take this issue further by looking at the effects of early tracking by comparing school outcomes at primary school (examined through PIRLS) with outcomes at age 15. They conclude that "Variation in performance, measured in a variety of ways, tends to increase across levels of schooling when a country employs early tracking. Although the evidence on the level of performance is more mixed, there is very little evidence that there are efficiency gains associated with this increased inequality". Bauer and Riphahn (2005), analysing data from Switzerland (where the age of first tracking differs across cantons), found that early tracking reinforces the relative advantage of children of highly educated parents if compared to children of parents with low level of education. Drawing on this evidence, a Communication of the European Commission argues that tracking should be postponed to upper secondary level (Council of the European Union, 2006; Commission of the European Communities, 2006).

There are also experiences where individual school systems have abolished early tracking:

● Meghir and Palme (2005) showed that Swedish reform in the 1950s, which replaced tracking at age 12 with a comprehensive system, increased attainment overall and helped equity by generating particularly sharp improvements for students with unskilled fathers.

● Under a 2002 reform of the Polish education system, selection between academic and vocational tracks was postponed from the age of 14 to 15. When data from PISA 2000 and PISA 2003 are compared, this reform appears to have both increased average performance and reduced inequity. (An alternative hypothesis is that delaying tracking by one year delays, but does not remove, a one-off downward impact on performance of a school transition.)

● Pekkarinen *et al.* (2006) showed that Finnish school reform in the 1970s, which postponed tracking from age 11 to age 16 and introduced a uniform curriculum in lower secondary schools, improved equity by reducing the earnings correlation between fathers and sons.

The existence of early tracks may create other risks for equity. Resources are one issue. For example Oakes *et al.* (1992) showed that in high schools in the United States, better teachers and more resources are often assigned to more academic and prestigious tracks. Pedagogy is another issue. In systems employing early tracking, students report that their mathematics teachers are generally *less* likely to show interest in individual student learning (OECD, 2004d). In comprehensive systems, the heterogeneity of the classroom encourages attention to individual learning needs. Chapter 4 provides examples of different approaches in this area.

There is much less evidence on the effect of streaming within schools, but PISA 2003 shows that where ability grouping in mathematics classes is avoided, there is better overall performance (OECD, 2004b).

To explore whether the construction of the education system tends to reinforce or weaken the impact of students' background on achievement, some national systems (France and Australia, for example) monitor the flow through various pathways of students from different backgrounds. But in other systems (in Spain, for example) there is limited monitoring. Very limited monitoring can conceal problems of access and transition, taking the pressure off institutions and transferring the problem to individuals to solve on their own.

3.3. Designing an inclusive upper secondary education system

The design of education systems can either increase or diminish initial inequities. Key factors for success include effective transitions from one level to the next (points at which students at risk may fall out of the system), attractive alternatives to mainstream upper secondary education, bridges from one educational track to another and second chance education.

Box 3.1. **Who knows how things would have turned out?**

An intelligent but rebellious teenager with a turbulent home life, Sarah began falling behind in attendance and class work in her freshman year. Like many other 15-year-olds, she had a talent for making poor decisions. She and her friends would often skip out of school after lunch and cruise up and down Broadway. Teachers rarely stopped them, but school authorities knew what she and her friends were up to. One morning Sarah went to the school office to discuss getting back on track but got a surprise. One of the administrators asked her point-blank, "Why don't you just quit school?" "I was just a kid", says Sarah with a laugh. "It was like they said the magic words. So I told them, 'O.K.!' And I left."

Sarah never set foot in a high school again. She got her GED, but now she's too afraid to try community college, she says, because she doesn't want to look stupid. Although she has a house she owns with her husband and a fine job serving coffee, biscuits and small talk at Ole McDonald's Cafe in nearby Acton, Ind., Sarah is not without regret. "It would have been nice to have someone pushing me to stay", she says. "Who knows how things would have turned out?"

Source: "Dropout Nation", *Time Magazine*, 17 April 2006.

Completing basic education and improving transitions

The successful completion of basic (lower secondary) education remains a challenge in some OECD countries and for some groups. For example, in 2001, in New Zealand (16%), Portugal (29%), Mexico (33%) and Turkey (47%), a high proportion of 20-to-24-year-olds did not successfully complete lower secondary school – meaning either that they left early or did not obtain a leaving certificate (OECD, 2006b). In Spain in 2001, about 25% of children failed to obtain their leaving certificate from lower secondary education. Sometimes a compulsory school diploma may be required to enrol in upper secondary school. Countries address this issue in different ways. In Slovenia, students who complete at least seven years of nine-year elementary school may continue their education in a short-term vocational education programme and move to more demanding secondary school programmes (Flere, 2004). The Spanish *Social Guarantee* programme provides good employment opportunities for youngsters who have not successfully completed basic education although it does not lead to a formal qualification. Students are not awarded a formal degree and, over the long run, they may have difficulty moving to upper secondary education and integrating into the labour market (Teese *et al.*, 2005).

Transitions involve many changes for a student: a new school, a new track or programme, and new colleagues and teachers. Such changes can precipitate dropout.[1] Given academic selection, some youngsters might not meet the formal requirements to obtain a place in the school of their choice. In Switzerland for example, completing compulsory education is a necessary condition but not always sufficient to obtain an apprenticeship position. Moreover, some students – many with immigrant backgrounds – are not able to enrol for any form of education or training after completing lower secondary education (Coradi Vellacott and Wolter, 2004).

Countries have different strategies to support students at transition points. In Sweden and Finland, students who would like to improve their grades and skills are offered special programmes at the end of lower secondary school (see Box 3.2).

Box 3.2. **Parallel secondary education completion programmes in selected countries**

In the Finnish special course of study, students may stay one additional year in comprehensive school and follow a special course of study. In 2002, 35% of students who chose this option were enrolled in general education, 48% were enrolled in vocational programmes, 3% were working and 2% were unemployed or in other activities (Grubb et al., 2005).

The individual programme in Sweden is designed for students who lack the entrance requirements for upper secondary school, and aims to return them to mainstream education. In 2002, pupils enrolled in individual programmes represented 7% of all pupils in upper secondary school, with an overrepresentation of students with immigrant background (about 40% compared to 15% for all programmes). But the outcomes of the programme were modest. Four years after graduating from compulsory school, half of those who received remedial tuition in year 9 had dropped out of their upper secondary studies (Swedish National Agency for Education, n.d.).

France has a programme (les dispositifs relais) which aims to reintegrate disaffected students at lower secondary level into either general or vocational formal education. Of the students attending classes relais in 2000/01, 80% integrated into mainstream schools or found employment (Ministry of National Education, Higher Education and Research, France, 2004).

In the United States, Early College High Schools (recently created to combine upper secondary education with some tertiary education courses) have been successful in reducing dropout. However, it is not clear whether the decrease has been in response to the combination of upper secondary and tertiary courses or to other important elements of the programme (see Box 3.3).

Box 3.3. **The Early College High School Initiative in the United States**

This initiative, supported by the Bill & Melinda Gates Foundation, aims to improve high school completion rates and increase the number of students transferring to college, especially for low-income students, black Americans and those for whom English is not their native language. These schools are small (maximum 400 students) and aim to help students earn their high school diploma and obtain two-year college credits allowing access to university education. Each student has a personalised learning plan and receives support from advisors and teachers in and out of school through a longer school day, Saturday school, and summer school. Parents and community are also involved in the programme.

These institutions have met with some difficulties, including a demanding curriculum and varying levels of academic and social skills among students who enrol. The challenge is to provide weaker learners with support while maintaining standards. In response, some schools in the scheme have introduced a minimum requirement entry exam – a selection tool which may pose problems to equity. In addition, teacher turnover has been particularly important in schools where students' success depends strongly on student-teacher relationships.

First evaluation results suggest positive impacts on attendance, academic engagement and self-esteem, completion rate from high school, and transition to post-secondary school. At one school in Ferndale, Washington near an Indian reservation (the Lummi Nation Reservation), dropout rates decreased after the school joined Early College High School Initiative in 2004 – from 69% in 2002 to 16% in 2004/05. There are plans to establish more than 170 Early College High Schools by 2008.

Source: American Institute for Research, 2006; Hoffman, 2003; Centre for Native Education, n.d.; The Early College High School Initiative, n.d.; Wolk, 2005.

Equivalent alternatives: vocational and other pathways

Some people drop out because they find traditional styles of academic learning unappealing. Attractive and constructive alternatives in secondary education may therefore help provide more opportunities for these students and reduce dropout. The principle of equivalence aims to reconcile equality and diversity: equal levels of education should in principle have equal value and impact on people's opportunities (for example, in terms of access to labour market positions or further and tertiary education). The aim is that *all* children complete the equivalent of upper secondary school and that *all* have the opportunity to pursue tertiary studies if they so desire (Nicaise *et al.*, 2005). This strategy requires better guidance and counselling for students; improving the quality of vocational education and training (VET) and other options; and, as alternatives to more academic pathways, courses which offer easier transitions to the world of work. Education systems must offer strong incentives for learning and ensure that these incentives are understood by all students, including those with the weakest achievement. Without clear demonstrable benefits, early school leaving and under-achievement will continue.

Traditionally, vocational education and training have catered to students of lower socio-economic background and/or lower academic achievement, particularly in some countries (Arum and Shavit, 1994). In the period of educational expansion, "vocational education enabled the educational systems to absorb disadvantaged groups at the secondary level without disturbing the basic social interests of advantaged groups at higher levels in the school system." (Blossfeld and Shavit, 1993) In fact, in countries which participated in the Thematic Review on Equity in Education (such as Sweden, Finland, Norway and Hungary), VET students are particularly subject to dropout when compared with students in academic tracks. Conversely, because of its practical orientation, VET may help to engage students who dislike more academic learning. Arum and Shavit (1994) argue that vocational education can become a safety net for these students, since VET can provide practical labour market skills to less academically inclined students. A between-countries comparison (Figure 3.4) shows that countries with higher

Figure 3.4. **Some countries with larger VET systems have lower dropout rates (2001, 2002)**

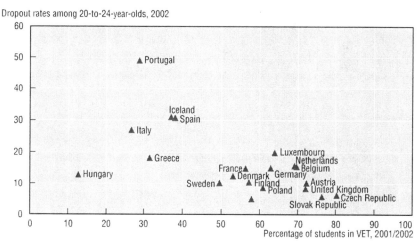

Source: OECD (2005e), *From Education to Work: A Difficult Transition for Young Adults with Low Levels of Education,* OECD, Paris; Eurydice.

percentages of students in VET tend also to have lower dropout rates (correlation –0.60, significant). However, these results are difficult to interpret.

Many countries are seeking to make VET more attractive in both content and quality in order to retain students in education and training and improve their access to upper secondary academic programmes or tertiary education. A more flexible curriculum may help make VET more attractive and reduce dropout rates. In a longitudinal study of 22 non-selective government high schools in New South Wales (Australia), Ainley and Sheret (1992) report that a wider curriculum based on alternative programmes improves students' progression. DeLuca *et al.*, (2005) find that among students in vocational education (at the statutory age when entering high school), dropout decreases when students follow both academic and vocational courses. The review team that visited Spain points out that "links between academic and vocational studies have great pedagogical importance. A rigid separation between

---

Box 3.4. **VET Reforms to improve equity and quality**

Sweden and Norway have reformed upper secondary education in an attempt to improve the quality of VET. Both countries have flexible secondary systems without dead ends, with all tracks (academic as well as vocational) allowing access to tertiary education. In Norway, students can choose between equally respected strands of courses in general academic and vocational/technical fields. The curriculum followed by all students in upper secondary school combines theoretical knowledge with vocational training, although according to recent estimates by Statistics Norway, the dropout rate in Norway is still high (around 23%).

The Swedish VET system has 17 different equivalent upper secondary programmes, including 3 academic and 14 vocational. All vocational courses have been supplemented by theoretical subjects. In Sweden, however, there are high dropout rates from upper secondary education.[1] One possibility is that the new vocational courses are too difficult and too long for less academically oriented students. As we know, the impact of VET reform on dropout rates has not been yet examined.[2]

In addition, many countries, including Finland, France, Spain and Switzerland, have created direct pathways from upper secondary vocational education to vocational tertiary education.

1. In Sweden, the VET system was reformed at the beginning of the 1990s. The duration of studies was extended from two to three years, the VET curriculum was completed with theoretical subjects and assessment methods were changed.
2. Ekstrom (2003) analysed the impact of the third year in vocational upper secondary education on the enrolment in tertiary education and on the employment rate. She observed a positive impact of the new VET on participation in tertiary education and null or negative impact on employment opportunities.

NO MORE FAILURES: TEN STEPS TO EQUITY IN EDUCATION – ISBN 978-92-64-03259-0 – © OECD

academic and vocational prevents them from being exploited, and contributes to higher rates of failure." (Teese *et al.*, 2005)

Some countries are allowing students to transfer between general and vocational courses and to obtain key skills and competences in modular form, regardless of the track or stream. In Flemish Belgium, students can choose between vocational and general courses and receive both vocational qualifications and diplomas of general studies giving access to tertiary education. In the 1990s, Finland piloted an approach in which students were given the option of choosing courses at both general and vocational upper secondary school. The success of this experiment was rather limited; few students earned double qualifications. One limitation of this programme was that the students involved received rather weak counselling and guidance in how to go about developing their own courses of study (Grubb *et al.*, 2005).

Guidance and counselling

Some young people may find themselves in programmes they are not interested in, either because of inadequate results for their preferred option, insufficient information or because they were not ready to make an occupational choice at the critical moment.[2] In Finland, for example, lack of interest in the field of study is one of the factors contributing to early school leaving (Grubb *et al.*, 2005).

In principle, guidance and counselling services should help students to make educational and career choices. But the quality and adequacy of counselling varies enormously, and support for potential dropouts from school is often inadequate (Mortimore *et al.*, 2005). Career guidance tends to be more focused on educational decision making than on occupational choice and this disadvantages students in VET. An OECD study on career and guidance found that in Belgium (Flanders), Finland, Hungary, Norway and Switzerland, students in vocational upper secondary school received less individual career counselling than those pursuing academic studies (OECD, 2004c).

Guidance and counselling services need to engage more fully with the world of work in order to provide students with the opportunity to try out future professions. Practical options include visits and meetings with representatives of local industries, community agencies, work simulation or work placements (OECD, 2004c). In Norway, for example, guidance and counselling are a part of the curriculum from the primary education stage onward. At lower secondary level, pupils may spend at least one week at a workplace.

Better links to the world of work

Strong links with employers help to ensure that the skills acquired through VET correspond to labour market requirements, most directly through the involvement of employers in the design of occupational qualifications (OECD, 2000). In Ireland, through the School Completion Programme, the government has launched a schools-business partnership to support educational inclusion, which has apparently reduced dropout (National Economic and Social Forum, 2002).

Good quality apprenticeship training may reduce early school leaving and assist integration into the labour force (OECD, 2000). In France, the particularly disadvantaged students who tend to opt for apprenticeships are more likely to find a job than those with school-based vocational education (Schütz and Wössmann, 2006). Apprenticeship is also considered a valuable option for disadvantaged students in Norway (Leney, 2005).

In German-speaking countries (such as Austria, Germany and Switzerland) and in Denmark, there is a dual system which combines practical training obtained through workplace apprenticeships with more academic education in school. Students are trained in state-recognised occupations. In these countries, a higher proportion of the cohort enters VET. For example, in the German-speaking part of Switzerland, 80% of students are enrolled in vocational education (OECD, 2005f). But changes in the labour market driven by technological innovation have also affected countries with the dual system. Some traditional trades and crafts are threatened, either by relocation of the work outside OECD countries, or simply because the work can now be performed by a machine.

3.4. Removing dead ends and providing second chances

Young people mature at different rates, both intellectually and emotionally, sometimes in stops and starts. This means that it is extremely important to provide a second chance for those who want to return to education later in life. For the same reason, it is important to eliminate dead ends in the education system – pathways which lock people out of further learning options. A flexible adult learning system can be a strong alternative. It should take into consideration working and family life, previous (sometimes negative) educational experience and recognise that adults may have skills and knowledge gained outside formal education processes. In Sweden, where the effect of parental social origin on educational attainment has weakened significantly (Shavit and Blossfeld, 1993; Breen *et al.*, 2005), Erikson and Jonsson (1996) argue that, along with low poverty rates and comprehensive schools, well-developed second chances in the Swedish education system help to yield this outcome.

Adult learning institutions and practices

Adult learning takes place in a diversity of institutions: institutions designed specifically for adults, folk high schools, community colleges, one-stop shops, community centres, enterprise-based training centres and regular educational institutions that open up to adults in the evenings or on weekends. Flexible learning arrangements, including part-time or distance learning, reduce the opportunity cost of studying by making it compatible with everyday adult lives. Provision needs to be targeted to meet specific adults' needs and schedules. Otherwise, there are no incentives for dropouts to return to an experience in which they had already failed once (see Box 3.5).

Box 3.5. **Adult learning institutions in different countries**

Finland has over 260 adult education centres. Originally created for adult vocational training, they evolved to offer learning opportunities for the entire adult population. There are general upper secondary schools for adults, where they can complete basic and general upper secondary education and take the matriculation examination and also study individual subjects, mainly languages.

In Sweden, municipal adult education centres (*Komvux*) are widespread and play an important role in providing compulsory and upper secondary level education for adults. These centres were the main focus of the recent Adult Education Initiative to provide upper secondary education to adults who lacked it.

In Spain, most public adult learning is provided in adult education centres run by autonomous regional governments, municipalities or local authorities, and it includes both formal and non-formal education.

In Mexico, the Community Halls (*Plazas Comunitarias*) allow disadvantaged youths and adults access to basic education and work training opportunities through three learning environments: a regular classroom; an educational television and video room; and a computer room with Internet connections. Because of the lack of learning provision and basic information, the Community Halls have proved extremely important to the life of the communities. With their one-stop-shop approach, they have been effective in bringing in reluctant learners, and providing access to ICT for adults.

In Australia, Technical and Further Education Colleges (TAFE) are open to students who do not have a lower secondary school certificate. For unemployed people, the aboriginal population or people from a non-English speaking background, there are special courses to help them enter or return to the workforce. Students may obtain recognition for prior learning and design a study schedule that meets their needs. Services include tutorial support, career and counselling advice, childcare centres, student associations and libraries. All TAFE courses are nationally recognised and qualifications considered valid by employers and training organisations throughout Australia.

Source: OECD, 2005d; TAFE New South Wales.

For basic educational attainment, most OECD countries have institutions that cater to adults by providing literacy training, and primary and secondary education. The recognition of prior learning (RPL) can stimulate those who dropped out to obtain recognition for some of their skills and knowledge gained outside formal education (for example in the workplace) and use that recognition to support completion of their studies. The workplace can also be a venue for basic education credentials and skill development (OECD, 2005d). Adults make use of these opportunities in countries where they are available. In Sweden for example, at least 28% of all young people admitted into tertiary education had passed through *Komvux* (municipal adult education) or Liberal adult education (Nicaise *et al.*, 2005).

Potentially, a second chance system can encourage dropout in initial upper secondary education, by reducing the costs and risks to the students involved. This may represent flexibility in lifelong learning, but it could also generate some inefficiencies. In Sweden, some students drop out of mainstream schools into second chance institutions (where grades are apparently easier) in order to increase their chances of access to tertiary education.

Box 3.6. **Work-based learning initiatives for the employed and the unemployed**

Some work-based initiatives are aimed at young unemployed dropouts. A French programme (*Mission générale d'insertion de l'éducation nationale*), helps students to obtain basic skills.

In Finland, students disaffected from conventional upper secondary education can enrol in workshop programmes that can lead to vocational qualifications.

In Slovenia, young unemployed dropouts may participate in a project entitled Learning for Young Adults, designed to motivate them to resume their interrupted schooling and to offer them individual support in acquiring basic skills while they compensate for prior knowledge gaps.

In the United Kingdom, the Employer Training Pilots (ETPs) encourage employees to obtain basic and higher skills by offering paid time off to employees and wage subsidies to employers. ETPs typically provide free information and advice and free learning for employees who do not have higher skills. For courses on literacy and numeracy, all employees can participate. Over 80 000 trainees and 11 000 employers are currently engaged in the programme. Three-quarters of these trainees left school at or before age 16 and most had no recognised qualifications.

Source: Ministry of National Education, Higher Education and Research, France, 2004; Grubb *et al.*, 2005; Flere, 2004; Department for Work and Pensions, UK, 2004.

Recognition of prior learning

Recognition of prior learning (RPL) involves formal recognition of skills and knowledge gained outside formal education (for example in the workplace) and uses that recognition to support further education. It can reduce total learning time and may encourage workers to participate in learning. Recognition mechanisms vary, but some systems provide partial credits toward a formal qualification; others provide some type of formal recognition or degree that is accepted in society. There are no common standards in the skills recognition process. A variety of assessment methods such as informal interviews and testing are used, either individually or in combination.

Table 3.2. **Selected approaches to recognition of prior learning**[1]

	Initiative	How many participate
France	Every person who can demonstrate at least three months of professional experience can apply for official recognition of this experience (la validation des acquis de l'expérience – VAE). There is no exam; the assessment is made by the commission on the basis of proofs submitted by the candidate. All legally recognised certifications, qualifications and titles can be obtained through VAE (Le Centre INFO website: www.centre-inffo.fr).	In 2005, 21 379 persons sought recognition of prior experience and 88% of them were successful. Of the total number of candidates, the share of those unemployed and inactive was 26% (ministère de la Jeunesse, de l'Éducation nationale et la Recherche, Direction de l'évaluation et de la prospective, France).
Norway	Adults born before 1978 who have not completed upper secondary education have the right to have their non-formal learning assessed and to take a shortened course of education based on their previous experience.	10 000 adults have their competences validated in upper secondary education each year from a total number of around 20 000 adults participating in upper secondary education.
Portugal	The national system of recognition, validation and certification of competencies (Sistema Nacional de Reconhecimento, Validação e Certificação de Competências, RVCC) targets low-skilled active adults, both unemployed and employed, and allows for recognition of prior learning. It enables under-qualified adults to improve their employability and encourages their return, at any time, to education and training processes.	More than 35 000 participants, of whom 12 707 obtained qualifications between 2001 and 2003.
United States	The General Educational Development (GED) exams include norm-referenced tests in writing, social studies, science, reading and mathematics. Individuals who successfully pass all five exams earn a GED credential, which is generally intended to serve as an alternative to a high school diploma.	Between 400 000 and 700 000 US residents pass the GED annually.

1. Information about OECD's work on recognition of non-formal and informal learning is available at www.oecd.org/edu/recognition.

3.5. Summary conclusions and recommendations

The design of education systems and the pathways through those systems can help or hinder equity. A fair and inclusive system needs to manage the extent of differentiation, by postponing tracking to at least the later teenage years and seeking to avoid social separation between different types of schools. It must remove dead ends, offer second chances, and provide guidance throughout the transitions involved.

Step 1: Limit early tracking and streaming and postpone academic selection

Evidence

- Secondary school systems with large social differences between schools tend on average to have worse results in mathematics and reading and a greater spread of reading outcomes. Social background is more of an obstacle to educational success than in systems where there are not large socio-economic differences between schools.

- Academic selection by school systems is associated with great social differences between schools and a stronger effect of socio-economic status on performance, but also with a stronger performance at the top end of the scale in mathematics and science.

- Evidence on secondary students from PISA (OECD's Programme for International Student Assessment) compared to evidence at primary level from PIRLS (Progress in International Reading Literacy Study) and evidence from countries which have introduced comprehensive schooling suggest that early tracking is associated with reduced equity in outcomes and sometimes weakens results overall.

Policy recommendations

- *Early tracking and streaming* need to be justified in terms of proven benefits as they very often pose risks to equity.

- School systems using *early tracking* should consider raising the age of first tracking to reduce inequities and improve outcomes.

- *Academic selection* needs to be used with caution since it too poses risks to equity.

Step 2: Manage school choice so as to contain the risks to equity

Evidence

- School choice may pose risks to equity since well-educated parents may make shrewder choices. Better-off parents have the resources to exploit choice, and academic selection tends to accelerate the progress of those who have already gained the best start in life from their parents.

NO MORE FAILURES: TEN STEPS TO EQUITY IN EDUCATION – ISBN 978-92-64-03259-0 – © OECD

- Across countries, greater choice in school systems is associated with larger differences in the social composition of different schools (see Figure 3.3).

Policy recommendations

- *School choice poses risks to equity* and requires careful management, in particular to ensure that it does not result in increased differences in the social composition of different schools.
- Given school choice, oversubscribed schools need ways to *ensure an even social mix in schools* – for example selection methods such as lottery arrangements. Financial premiums to schools attracting disadvantaged pupils may also help.

Step 3: In upper secondary education, provide attractive alternatives, remove dead ends and prevent drop out

Evidence

- Between 5% and 40% of students drop out of school in OECD countries (measured by the proportion of 20-to-24-year-olds not in education and without upper secondary education). They go on to have low skills and suffer high rates of unemployment.
- Among other factors, dropout stems from disenchantment with school, lack of support at home, negative learning experiences and repeating years.
- Early identification of students at risk helps to improve outcomes and prevent dropout.
- Good career guidance and counselling combined with a more flexible and diverse (and therefore attractive) curriculum help to reduce dropout rates.

Policy recommendations

- *Early prevention* of dropout is the best cure. Basic schooling should support and engage those who struggle at school as well as those who excel.
- *Monitoring* of those at risk (using information on attendance, performance and involvement in school activities) should be linked to interventions to improve outcomes and prevent dropout.
- *Upper secondary education* needs to be attractive not just to an academically inclined elite, offering good quality pathways without dead ends and effective links to the world of work.
- *Smooth transitions* prevent school failure and dropout. Additional learning support at the end of secondary school may help to encourage students to stay in school.

- *Good quality vocational tracks* are essential. Removing an academic hurdle from entrance to general upper secondary education and allowing access to tertiary education from vocational programmes, as Sweden and Norway have done, can increase the status of the vocational track.

Step 4: Offer second chances to gain from education

Evidence

- Those who fail at school often find it difficult to recover later on. In all OECD countries, those with weak basic qualifications are much less likely to continue learning in adult life (see Figure 2.5). Significantly, this figure also shows that there are big differences between countries.

- Across OECD countries, many adults and young dropouts without basic education obtain school qualifications through second chance programmes. In the United States, almost 60% of dropouts eventually earn a high school credential (GED certificate).

Policy recommendations

- *Second chances are necessary* for those who lack basic education and skills. These include programmes that provide literacy training, primary and secondary education, work-based programmes and arrangements to recognise informal learning.

ANNEX 3.A

Annex 3.A1. **Correlation coefficients between separation index and PISA outcomes**

	Maths	Science	Reading
Mean score	−0.40 *	−0.30 NS	−0.48**
Top achievers %	−0.17 NS	−0.2 NS	−0.43*
Low achievers %	0.45*	0.3 NS	0.47**
Standard deviation	0.35 NS	−0.07 NS	0.18 NS

Annex 3.A2. **Regression analysis: Effects of selection by ability on different measures**

	Dependent variable	Observations	Multiple R-squared		Estimated coefficient	t Statistic
3.2.1	Percentage of top achievers (Level 6) on PISA mathematics scale	27 OECD countries + Russia	0.40	Intercept X variable: Selection by ability	2.88 0.04*	4.37 2.26
	Percentage of top achievers (above 600 points) on PISA science scale	27 OECD countries + Russia	0.38	Intercept X variable: Selection by ability	14.4 0.11*	7.67 2.11
	Percentage of top achievers (above 625 points) on PISA reading scale	27 OECD countries + Russia	0.10	Intercept X variable: Selection by ability	8.52 −0.02 NS	7.50 −0.54
3.2.2	Impact of SES on academic performance	27 OECD countries	0.47	Intercept X variable: Selection by ability	38.61 0.13*	20.92 2.65
3.3.3	Index of separation	28 OECD countries + Russia	0.48	Intercept X variable: Selection by ability	0.21 0.001*	11.64 2.88
3.3.4	Index of separation	28 OECD countries + Russia	0.48	Intercept X variable: Selection by ability X variable: Selection by ability	0.21 0.001* 0.001 NS	11.64 2.88 1.12

Note: * significant at 5% level, ** significant at 1% level, NS not significant.
Source: OECD (2004b), *Learning for Tomorrow's World: First Results from PISA 2003*, Paris.

Notes

1. In an Irish report on dropouts, transfer from primary to secondary level was described as a key concern with regard to early school leaving (National Economic and Social Forum, 2002).

2. See Figure 5.20 on the first age of selection in education systems in OECD (2004b), *Learning for Tomorrow's World: First Results from PISA 2003*, OECD, Paris.

References

Ainley, J. and M. Sheret (1992) "Progress through High School: A Study of Senior Secondary Schooling in New South Wales", ACER *Research Monograph*, No. 43. ACER, Hawthorn, Victoria, Australia.

American Institute for Research, SRI International (2006), *Early College High School Initiative. 2003-2005 Evaluation Report*, prepared for the Bill & Melinda Gates Foundation, American Institute for Research, 2006.

Arum, R. and Y. Shavit (1994), "Another Look at Tracking, Vocational Education and Social Reproduction", *European University Institute Working Paper*, No. 94/1, European University Institute, Florence.

Bauer, P. and R. Riphahn (2005), "Timing of School Tracking as a Determinant of Intergenerational Transmission of Education", *Economics Letters 91* (2006), Elsevier, pp. 90-97.

Bjorklund, A., P.A. Edin, P. Fredriksson and A. Krueger (2004), *Education, Equality, and Efficiency: An Analysis of Swedish School Reforms during the 1990s*, Institute for Labour Market Policy Evaluation, Uppsala.

Blossfeld H. and Y. Shavit (eds.) (1993), *Persistent Inequalities: A Comparative Study of Educational Attainment in Thirteen Countries*, Westview Press, Boulder Colorado.

Bobbitt, L. and L. Horn (2000), "Mapping the Road to College: First-Generation Students' Math Track, Planning Strategies, and Context of Support", *Statistical Analysis Report*, March 2000, National Centre for Education Statistics, US Department of Education, Office of Educational Research and Improvement.

Breen, R., R. Luijk, W. Muller and R. Pollak (2005), "Non-Persistent Inequality in Educational Attainment: Evidence from Eight European Countries", Paper presented for the meeting of Research Committee 28 (ISA) *Inequality and Mobility in Family, School, and Work*, Los Angeles, August 18-21, 2005.

Brunello, G., M. Gianni and K. Ariga (2004), "The Optimal Timing of School Tracking", Institute for the Study of Labor (IZA) *Discussion Paper*, No. 995.

Centre for Native Education (n.d.), Antioch University, Seattle, *www.antiochsea.edu/about/cne*.

Commission of the European Communities (2006), Communication from the Commission to the Council and to the European Parliament, *Efficiency and Equity in European Education and Training Systems*, SEC(2006)1096.

Council of the European Union (2006), *Conclusions of the Council and the Representatives of the Governments of the Member States*, Meeting within the Council on Efficiency and Equity in Education and Training, 15 November 2006.

Coradi Vellacott, M. and S.Wolter (2004), *Equity in the Swiss Education System: Dimensions, Causes and Policy Responses, National Report from Switzerland contributing* to the OECD's *Review of Equity in Education*, Swiss Coordination Center for Research in Education.

DeLuca, S., A. Estacion and S. Plank (2005), *Dropping Out of High School and the Place of Career and Technical Education: A Survival Analysis of Surviving High School*, National Dissemination Center for Career and Technical Education, Columbus, Ohio.

Department for Work and Pensions, UK (2004), *OECD Thematic Review of Adult Learning in the United Kingdom – Background Report*.

Dronkers, J. and P. Robert (2003), "Effectiveness of Public and Private Schools in a Comparative Perspective", Paper for the Sociology of Education Regular Session: International Perspectives on the Sociology of Education at the Annual Meeting of the American Sociological Association in San Francisco, 14-17 August 2004, European University Institute, Department of Political Sciences.

Ekström, E. (2003), "Earning Effects of Adult Secondary Education in Sweden", Institute for Labour Market Policy Evaluation (IFAU), Working Paper, 2003:16, Uppsala.

Erikson, R. and J. Jonsson (eds.) (1996), *Can Education be Equalized: The Swedish Case in Comparative Perspective*, Westview Press, Boulder, Colorado.

European Journal of Education Research, Development and Policies, "Attitudes, Choice and Participation – Dimensions of the Demand for Schooling" (2006), Vol. 41, No. 1.

Eurydice (1994), *Measures to Combat Failure at School: A Challenge for the Construction of Europe, www.eurydice.org*.

Eurydice (1997), *Measures Taken in the Member States of the European Union to Assist Young People who Have Left the Education Without Qualification, www.eurydice.org*.

Eurydice, *The Information Network on Education in Europe, www.eurydice.org*.

Fitz, J., S. Gorard and C. Taylor (2001), "Explaining School Segregation", Paper presented to British Educational Research Association (BERA) Annual Conference, University of Leeds, 13-15 September 2001, Cardiff University School of Social Sciences.

Flere, S. (2004), *Educational Equity and Inequity in Slovenia: Country Analytical Report*.

Gibbons, S. and S. Machin (2001), "Valuing Primary Schools", *Centre for the Economics of Education* (CEE), *Discussion Papers*, No. 0015, London School of Economics and Political Science.

Grubb N., S. Field, H. Marit Jahr and J. Neumüller (2005), *Equity in Education Thematic Review: Finland Country Note*, OECD, Paris, *www.oecd.org/dataoecd/49/40/36376641.pdf*.

Hanushek, E.A. and L. Wössmann (2005), "Does Educational Tracking Affect Performance and Inequality? Differences-in-Differences Evidence Across Countries", *Working Paper* No. 1415, Center for Economic Studies and Institute for Economic Research (CESifo), University of Munich.

Hanushek, E.A., J.F. Kain, J.M. Markman and S.G. Rivkin (2001), "Does Peer Ability Affect Student Achievement?", *Working Paper 8502*, National Bureau of Economic Research, Cambridge, MA.

Hoffman, N. (2003), "College Credit in High School: Increasing Postsecondary Credential Rates of Underrepresented Students", *Change*, July/August 2003, *www.earlycolleges.org/Downloads/collegecredit.pdf*.

Hoffman, N., M.L. Ferreira, S. Field and B. Levin (2005), *Equity in Education Thematic Review: Hungary Country Note*, OECD, Paris.

83

Hoxby, C.M., (2002), "The Power of Peers", *Education Next*, No. 2, Summer 2002, Hoover Institution.

Istance, D. and A. Sliwka, (2006), "Choice, Diversity and 'Exit' in Schooling – A Mixed Picture", *European Journal of Education*, Vol. 41, No. 1, pp. 45-58.

Jenkins, S., J. Miclewright and S. Schnepf (2006), "Social Segregation in Secondary Schools: How Does England Compare with Other Countries?", *Institute for Social and Economic Research Working Paper 2006-02*.

Kim, T. and K. Pelleriaux (2004), *Equity in the Flemish Educational System: Country Analytical Report*, University of Antwerp.

Leney, T. (2005), *Achieving the Lisbon Goal: The Contribution of VET*, European Commission.

Meghir, C. and M. Palme (2005), "Educational Reform, Ability and Family Background", *American Economic Review*, Vol. 95, No. 1, pp. 414-424(11).

Ministry of Education, Russian Federation (2005), *Equity in Education: Country Analytical Report – Russia*.

Ministry of National Education, Higher Education and Research, France (2004), *L'équité dans l'éducation en France: Rapport de base national présenté dans le cadre de l'activité de l'OCDE*, Paris.

Mortimore, P., S. Field and B. Pont (2005), *Equity in Education Thematic Review: Norway Country Note*, OECD, Paris, *www.oecd.org/dataoecd/10/6/35892523.pdf*.

National Economic and Social Forum (2002), "Early School Leavers, Forum Report No. 24", The National Economic and Social Forum, Dublin.

Nicaise, I., G. Esping-Andersen, B. Pont and P. Tunstall (2005), *Equity in Education Thematic Review: Sweden Country Note*, OECD, Paris, *www.oecd.org/dataoecd/10/5/35892546.pdf*.

Oakes, J., M. Selvin, L.A. Karoly and G. Guiton (1992), *Educational Matchmaking: Academic and Vocational Tracking in Comprehensive High Schools*, Rand Report, Rand Corporation.

OECD (1994), *School: A Matter of Choice*, OECD, Paris.

OECD (2000), *From Initial Education to Working Life: Making Transition Work*, OECD, Paris.

OECD (2004b), *Learning for Tomorrow's World: First Results from PISA 2003*, OECD, Paris.

OECD (2004c), *Career Guidance and Public Policy: Bridging the Gap*, OECD, Paris.

OECD (2004d), *Completing the Foundation for Lifelong Learning: An OECD Survey of Upper Secondary Schools*, OECD, Paris.

OECD (2005c), *Education at a Glance: OECD Indicators 2005*, OECD, Paris.

OECD (2005d), *Promoting Adult Learning*, OECD, Paris.

OECD (2005e), *From Education to Work: A Difficult Transition for Young Adults with Low Levels of Education*, OECD, Paris.

OECD (2005f), *Country Report on National System Policies and Practices Concerning Children and Youth at Risk, Promoting Partnership for Inclusion – Switzerland*, OECD, CERI, Paris.

OECD (2005g), *School Factors Related to Quality and Equity: Results from PISA 2000*, OECD, Paris.

OECD (2006b), *Publicly Provided Goods and the Distribution of Resources*, OECD, Directorate for Employment, Labour and Social Affairs, OECD, Paris.

OECD (2006f), *Public Spending Efficiency: Questionnaire on the Pre-Primary, Primary and Lower Secondary Education Sector,* OECD/ECO, unpublished.

Pekkarinen, T., S. Pekkala and R. Uusitalo (2006), "Education Policy and Intergenerational Income Mobility: Evidence from the Finnish Comprehensive School Reform", *IZA Discussion Paper,* No. 2204

Schütz, G. and L. Wössmann (2006), *Efficiency and Equity in European Education and Training Systems prepared by the European Expert Network in Economics in Education to accompany the Communication and Staff Working Paper by the European Commission under the same title, http://ec.europa.eu/education/policies/2010/doc/eenee.pdf.*

Swedish National Agency for Education (n.d.), Official statistics of Sweden, Stockholm, *www.skolverket.se/sb/d/356.*

Swiss Contribution to Eurybase – the Information Database on Education Systems in Europe (2001), Information Documentation Education Suisse, Berne, *www.edk.ch/ PDF_Downloads/Bildungswesen_CH/Eurydice_00e.pdf.*

TAFE (Technical and Further Education) New South Wales, *www.tafensw.edu.au.*

Teese, R., P. Aasen, S. Field and B. Pont (2005), *Equity in Education Thematic Review: Spain Country Note,* OECD, Paris, *www.oecd.org/dataoecd/41/39/36361409.pdf.*

The Early College High School Initiative, *www.earlycolleges.org.*

Wolk, R. (2005), *"It's Kind of Different": Student Experience in Two Early College High Schools, www.earlycolleges.org/Downloads/KindOfDifferent.pdf#search=%22wolk%20%22it's%20 kind%20 of%20different%22%22.*

ISBN 978-92-64-03259-0
No More Failures: Ten Steps to Equity in Education
© OECD 2007

Chapter 4

School and Out-of-school Practices

This chapter looks at classroom practices that affect equity along with out-of-school practices, particularly relationships between schools, parents and communities. Among different approaches, we highlight the need to reduce grade repetition in some countries, to develop approaches designed for the individual learner (including mixed ability teaching), and effective intervention strategies to support underperforming students or classrooms. Schools also need to reach out to homes of disadvantaged children, using strategies such as homework clubs and improved communication with parents to improve the out-of-school learning environment.

All children can point to what matters to them most about their school and their school work. They will tell you about their school, their class, their courses, their teachers, whether the teacher explains things well, whether they get help when they don't understand things. They will tell you how much homework they get, whether they get help from their parents, how their parents react when they do well or badly at school – whether they talk to the teacher for example. This chapter looks at this core business of learning both in the classroom and at home. It examines the challenges and explores how policy and practice in this area can be made fairer and more inclusive.

4.1. Equity in the classroom: interventions for those in need

When learning difficulties emerge in the classroom, the response can be of two quite distinct types. First, the children affected can be moved to a different learning environment, preserving the relative homogeneity of performance within the original classroom. Measures of this type include special education and tracking and streaming, discussed in Chapter 3. Another way of preserving an even level of attainment within each classroom is to require those who have fallen behind to repeat a year. Although this is, in a sense, another means of differentiation, similar to those discussed in the previous chapter, it is also a means of handling individual learning difficulties at classroom level and for that reason is discussed here. Other options imply different teaching and intervention approaches to tackle varying levels of attainment within the classroom. To underpin all these approaches, a commitment to equity needs to be built into the culture of the system, so that stakeholders think of every policy or practice in terms of what it can achieve for those who need most help, as well as for the stronger performers.

Repeating years

The requirement to repeat a year typically follows a formal or informal assessment of the student by the teacher towards the end of the school year, which suggests that the student has not adequately understood the material taught or reached the expected level of competence (although sometimes repetition reflects failure in only some subjects). Subsequently, either the school or the school, parents and student together agree that the student should repeat the year of study, with a view to the student catching up during the repeated year. Table 4.1 sets out the mechanisms involved in selected countries.

NO MORE FAILURES: TEN STEPS TO EQUITY IN EDUCATION – ISBN 978-92-64-03259-0 – © OECD

Table 4.1. **Year repetition in primary and lower secondary education**

	When? How many times?	Who decides?	According to which criteria?
Belgium (Flanders)	Each year may be repeated once.	The teacher or the teaching team and school head, consulting with the pupil and parents.	Tests and examinations results. Information from the Centre for Educational Guidance.
Finland	Repetition possible in principle, but rare in practice.		
France	*Primary* Repetition at the end of the cycle.	The *conseil des maîtres de cycle* (teaching team), on the recommendation of the pupil's teacher.	Educational performance measured against the objectives set for the end of each cycle.
	Lower secondary (collège) Repetition possible at the end of the year.	The *conseil de classe* on the basis of teachers' recommendations.	Acquisition of skills defined in the curriculum.
Hungary	*Pre-primary* Children may be held back for an extra year.	The educational guidance institution or an expert committee consulting parents and kindergarten staff.	Sufficient maturity to start school.
	Primary and lower secondary From the fourth grade, a maximum of three times.	School teaching staff.	• Marks in any subjects, except failure to reach the standard of foreign language skills in the first four grades. • Lesson attendance below the level defined by law. • Requests from parents and pupils.
Norway	Repetition possible in principle, but rare in practice.		
Slovenia		The teaching staff, on the recommendation of the home-class teacher's recommendation, after consultation with other teachers, school counsellors and pupil's parents.	Failure to pass all subjects at the end of the school year.
Spain	*Primary* Repetition at the end of the cycle (composed of a few grades), not more than once.	The head teacher and class teacher consulting other teachers, the local educational psychology team, the parents and the inspectors.	Educational performance measured against the objectives set for the end of each cycle.
	Lower secondary Students are assessed in every course. They can repeat each course just once.	The assessment team, formed by the teachers' team for every group of students, under the co-ordination of the form teacher.	Failure in more than two subjects.
Sweden	Repetition possible in principle, but rare in practice.		
Switzerland	*Pre-primary* Children may be held back for an extra year.		Sufficient maturity to start school.
	Primary If repetition does not lead to catch-up, a child is transferred to a special class or school.	Teaching staff, following consultation with parents.	Achievement during evaluation period.
	Lower secondary Repetition is possible only once. Then a student is transferred to the next lower school type/level.	Teaching staff, following consultation with parents.	Achievement during evaluation period.

Source: Eurydice; *Swiss Contribution to Eurybase – the Information Database on Education Systems in Europe* (2001), Information Documentation Education Suisse, Berne; and reports prepared for the Equity in Education Thematic Review (available at *www.oecd.org/edu/equity/equityineducation*).

In some countries, such as France, Luxembourg, Mexico and Spain, more than 20% of students have to repeat a grade in either primary or secondary education (see Figure 4.1). In these countries, year repetition is one of the main tools used to respond to individual weak performance. In other countries, such as Japan, Korea and the Nordic countries, repetition is very uncommon and may reflect illness or absence during one year.

Figure 4.1. **How many students repeat years in primary and lower secondary school?**[1]

Percentage of 15-year-olds who say they have repeated once or more (2003)

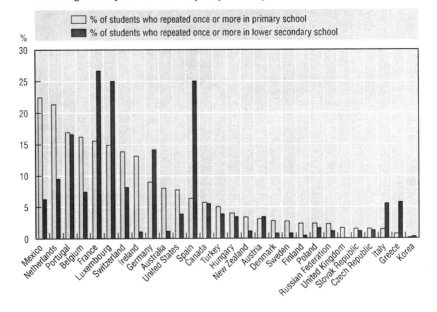

1. Data for Norway are missing. Year repetition is very rare in Norway.
Source: OECD, PISA 2003 Database.

Effectiveness and selection

Does repeating years help students to catch up? Unsurprisingly, those who repeat years tend to do badly at school. For example, they have much worse PISA results at age 15. In France, Paul and Troncin (2004) report that half of the pupils who repeat their first year at primary school go on to leave school with either no qualification or just a lower secondary qualification. Studies in Québec, Canada and the United States showed that those repeating years are much more likely to drop out of school later on. But these poor outcomes may reflect the fact that failing students are selected for repetition. How would they have performed had they been treated differently? In the absence of any randomised controlled trials, some studies compare outcomes for those who repeat years with others who are promoted despite poor results. Here again the studies suggest little benefit (Jimerson et al., 1997). Recent major reviews of international evidence (Paul, 1997; Paul and Troncin, 2004) conclude that the practice is ineffective, costly and stigmatising. One recent study concludes that "...over 50 years of educational research has failed to support any form of grade retention as an effective intervention for low achievement..." (Dalton et al., 2001).

Any effective approach to year repetition needs to select the right students. In any school grade, the ages of the children vary. For example, if school grades are determined by calendar year of birth, the youngest in each class will tend to be those born in December and the oldest those born in January. It is well established that school attainment, even in secondary school, is partially dependent on precise age, so if a fixed threshold of attainment is used to determine year repetition, the youngest in each year group will be most at risk. Repetition may therefore not distort the age mix of grades as much as might be expected; many of those repeating a year are only a few months older than those in the grade they are joining. Conversely many repeaters will not be weak performers, just young for their grade. Meanwhile, some older, genuinely weak performers will escape repetition. If the rationale for the measure is that it is designed to target weak performers, any selection procedure based on a fixed threshold of achievement will be flawed.

Research in both the United States and France also suggests that social background, independent of school attainment, is an important determinant of repeating. This may be due to behavioural difficulties associated with social background, or because educated parents are in a stronger position to oppose a repetition proposed by the school. Therefore the selection process may also pose risks for equity in terms of bias based on social background.

Costs and incentives

The costs of year repetition are substantial but indirect. Few estimates are available in the literature, although in the United States, Jimerson et al. (1997) estimated that for 1990 just the tuition cost would amount to USD 10 billion. On the assumption that year repetition implies a delay of one year in graduation, the costs will be one additional year of tuition falling to the public purse, plus the opportunity costs of one year of the student's time, which will mainly affect the student in the form of lower earnings – typically after a delay. Table 4.2 sets out some order-of-magnitude estimates of costs in selected countries for which data are available. These suggest that the cost per student per repeated year may be as much as USD 20 000 equivalent in New Zealand and total country cost could approach USD 450 million annually in Belgium.

Table 4.2. **Estimated costs of year repetition in selected countries**[1]

	Total country cost	Cost per student repeating one year Thousands USD at purchasing power parity	
	Primary and lower secondary school Millions USD at purchasing power parity	Primary school	Lower secondary school
Belgium	440	16	18
Denmark	30	14	14
Finland	10	8	11
Hungary	80	9	9
New Zealand	50	20	19
Sweden	40	10	10
United States	5 270	13	14

1. The cost of repetition is estimated as the sum of two components: the additional cost of tuition and the value of lost output. It is estimated separately for primary and lower secondary education. This assumes that repeating a year implies one more year in school than would otherwise have been the case. The year of reference is 2003. Tuition cost: Annual cost per student expressed in USD at purchasing power parity (PPP). Lost output: Estimated as the gross earnings of 15-to-24-year-olds, taking account of unemployment rates, expressed in USD at purchasing power parity. Total country costs are estimated by multiplying estimated costs per repeated year by the total number of repeaters.

Source: OECD (2005c), *Education at a Glance: OECD Indicators 2005*, OECD, Paris; OECD Education Database (2004).

Schools have very few incentives to take these large costs into account. Typically, extending students' time in education imposes additional tuition costs on the system as a whole by increasing the enrolled student population. But individual schools commonly receive their funding per student enrolled, so they will not have to absorb those increased costs or bear the opportunity costs of lost output. This is particularly important because alternative interventions to tackle learning difficulties, such as intensive help in small groups, very often have direct costs for schools.

Reducing repetition

In summary, year repetition tends to be relatively ineffective and costly, and schools have few incentives to take account of the costs. Repetition is sometimes defended on the grounds that it is necessary to maintain standards. Standards are important, but the standards that truly matter are concrete outcomes for students – not theoretical expectations for the level of students in particular classrooms. Some of the countries making little or no use of repetition have exceptionally high standards. Of course there may be individual cases where repeating a year may be helpful, but such cases are likely to be the exceptions. Countries are starting to change their practice. Luxembourg has recently introduced a reform to reduce the use of year repetition (Luxembourg, 2005), and in France the Council for School Evaluation has recommended a reduction in its use (*Haut Conseil de l'Évaluation de l'École*, 2004). In the course of this thematic review, expert teams made similar recommendations in Hungary and Spain (Hoffman *et al.*, 2005; Teese *et al.*, 2005) and some action has been taken in Spain.

Despite the evidence, year repetition remains common practice in some countries. There are two main reasons for this. First, studies in Belgium, Canada, France, Switzerland and the United States show that teachers widely support repetition and believe in its efficacy (Paul, 1997). This may be because teachers feel they lack the skills to teach a class with more diverse attainment levels. The second reason is that, at school level, as discussed, there are few incentives to take account of the costs.

This suggests two main policy conclusions. First, countries making extensive use of repetition need to explore with the teaching profession alternative ways of supporting those with learning difficulties in the

---

Box 4.1. **An alternative approach to year repetition in France**

One way to go about helping children who fall behind is to provide extra teaching time for them and adapt teaching to their needs. An example of a French secondary school situated in a disadvantaged area (les Ulis) shows how measures adapted to individual needs may benefit the most disadvantaged students. The school had a high year repetition rate and relatively weak results compared with other schools in the district. In 2004, the school proposed to students performing badly that they attend an experimental class instead of repeating a year. The objective was to improve student progression to the next grade, helping weaker students to catch up by giving them confidence in their learning capacities. The approach was based on a strengthening of the relationship between teacher and student, offering teaching more adapted to the individual student and encouraging students to participate actively: "*Les élèves ont enfin osé poser des questions concernant des savoir-faire même très simples. Cela leur a donc permis d'éclairer des zones d'ombre qui les empêchaient de progresser dans certaines matières. Dans aucune autre classe précédemment suivie, l'élève n'avait osé demander une telle explication quand la notion n'était pas maîtrisée.*" (Students became courageous enough to ask questions about how to do some very simple things. This allowed them to clear up shady areas which were blocking their progress in some subjects. In previous classes, students had not dared to ask for an explanation when they had not grasped the concept.) After one year in an experimental class students had more self-confidence and the rate of year repetition had decreased. This proved beneficial to the whole school as behavioural problems and truancy have diminished. (*Lycée de l'Essouriau*)

---

classroom. Alongside evidence that year repetition is ineffective, teachers need to be offered concrete alternatives. As discussed below, international experience suggests that such alternatives exist and that they can be very effective. Box 4.1 describes one successful initiative in France.

Second, school finance arrangements could usefully be adjusted, so that the real costs are more fully taken into account. One option would be to allow schools to retain any savings made from reductions in year repetition so that those savings could be used for other purposes. For example, schools could be funded according to the annual flow of students through from year of entry to year of graduation rather than based on enrolled school population. Reductions in year repetition would then yield lower class sizes or free up resources for other uses.

Measures within the classroom

Schools deal in many different ways with varying levels within a classroom or with students who are, or might be, falling behind. Overall, there needs to be a commitment to success for all students, reflected in high expectations and the organisation of programmes and approaches that allow for these expectations to be realised. It implies adapting teaching approaches to variations in attainment and providing additional support to those who might be underperforming. The classroom is the first place where learning difficulties can be detected and efficiently tackled. Flexible instruction, adapted to different levels of attainment is more challenging for teachers and it therefore needs to be underpinned by strong teacher preparation.

Most education systems have different methods of providing special help to those with learning difficulties, although they are not always well-evaluated. Here we will highlight a number of approaches for which there is some solid evidence of success. We will then give other examples where outcomes are less certain.

Within the classroom, there is good evidence that a family of techniques known as formative assessment leads to successful outcomes, particularly with underachieving students. Formative assessment is integrated into the teaching and learning process, so that information on student progress is used to identify gaps in understanding, and to shape teaching. It is therefore "formative" rather than "summative" assessment. Formative assessment also involves a change in the relationship between teacher and learner, ensuring that learners feel safe to reveal what they don't understand. In a review of research, Black and William (1998) conclude that the gains in achievement associated with formative assessment were "...among the largest ever reported for educational interventions". Several studies cited in the review also show that formative methods may be especially effective in helping underachieving students to succeed. In an OECD review of formative assessment in secondary classrooms (OECD, 2005h), describes several case study schools where large percentages of disadvantaged students had moved from failing to exemplary status over recent years. Programmes targeted at the needs of underachieving students also yielded positive results.

Teachers using formative assessment concentrate their attention on progress toward learning goals, rather than on the student's absolute level of attainment. Several studies show the value of this approach, noting that low achievers tend to attribute failure to low ability rather than lack of effort, and children develop ideas about their abilities and possibilities early in life (Black and William, 1998). Teachers using formative assessment can help students develop a collection of skills and strategies for learning that they can master over time, building their skills for learning to learn. For example, in one school in Newfoundland, Canada, ninth grade students read each other's research pieces in turn, using a scoring method to assess and improve the quality of written texts with regards to expression, structure, grammar and spelling. Students like the structured approach. One commented, "You can see what you did wrong and how you can fix it. It also makes it a lot easier to set aims for yourself." (OECD, 2005h)

The key elements in formative assessment are:

* a classroom culture that encourages interaction and the use of assessment tools;
* establishment of learning goals, and tracking of individual student progress toward those goals;
* use of varied instruction methods to meet diverse student needs;
* use of varied approaches to the assessment of student understanding;
* feedback on student performance and adaptation of instruction to meet identified needs;
* active involvement of students in the learning process.

Teachers' personalities and characteristics, or their varying expectations of different students, may also influence student performance. To avoid such biases, teachers at one school in Bari, Italy, discuss the interpretation of student results in teams. These teachers noted that the quality of their assessments has improved and they are able to bring potential biases to light (OECD, 2005h).

Reading Recovery programmes have also been effective. Reading Recovery is a short-term, intensive intervention of one-on-one lessons for low-achieving first graders. The intervention is used as a supplement to good classroom teaching. Individual students receive a half-hour lesson each school day for 12 to 20 weeks with a specially trained Reading Recovery teacher. As soon as students reach grade-level literacy expectations and

Box 4.2. **Tackling learning difficulties in Finland**

The first line of attack is the teacher, who is responsible for identifying students falling behind. The teacher works with such students one-on-one, or sometimes in groups of two to four, to correct the problem.

The second line of attack is the teacher's assistant, a person with some limited training who works under the direction of teachers. Sometimes the assistant sits beside a student, providing answers to questions and motivation for those whose attention flags. Sometimes the teacher's assistant works one-on-one or in small groups, always under the teacher's direction, on the material of the regular class and specific topics on which students need help.

The third line of attack is the qualified special needs teacher. Again, in consultation with the teacher, the special needs teacher works one-on-one or in small groups, with students who have not been adequately helped by the first two lines of attack. The special needs teachers usually concentrate on language (Finnish or Swedish) and on mathematics. Special education includes about 1.8% of students with severe disabilities who attend special schools, and another 4.4% with less serious disabilities who are mainstreamed. Both these groups are specifically diagnosed. A third group, around 20% of the cohort, are special needs students who have not been specifically diagnosed but simply need additional help to keep up.

A fourth approach is the multi-disciplinary team, for students whose weak progress is associated with wider home or social problems. The team consists of the teacher, the special needs teacher, the school's counsellor, and several individuals from outside the school – a psychologist, a social worker from the department of social services, representatives of the health and mental health systems as necessary, and individuals from the public housing system if that seems to be part of the problem.

Overall, these approaches to minimizing the number of students falling behind display two features: intensification (providing more time by more instructors) and alternative approaches (rather than "more of the same"), particularly through the efforts of special needs teachers and multi-disciplinary teams. But they do so in consistent ways, working with the classroom teacher on the specific subjects students are having trouble with, rather than relying on a grab bag of after-school programmes and tutoring efforts randomly distributed by grade levels and subjects.

The outcomes of this set of procedures (alongside other positive features of the Finnish education system) are remarkable. Only 1.1% of Finnish students were assessed as performing below Level 1 in reading in PISA 2003, compared with an OECD average of 6.7%. In other words, fully five-sixths of those who, by the standards of the OECD average, might have been expected to be very poor readers have achieved higher reading standards. The results for science and mathematics are nearly as good.

Source: Grubb et al., 2005, abridged quotation.

model of distributed leadership focusing on individual student performance (OECD, forthcoming).

- In Flanders, Belgium, extra teaching is provided to children who experience learning difficulties or who are otherwise disadvantaged. To qualify for extra teaching, a secondary school must have 10% target group students in the first grade of secondary education (age 12 to 14) and 25% in the second and third grades (age 14 to 18) who are living in economically and culturally unfavourable circumstances. To obtain the extra teaching support, schools have to give attention to five areas: prevention and remediation of developmental and learning disadvantages, Dutch language proficiency, intercultural education, socio-economic development and parental involvement. Interventions can involve follow up with individual students, differentiation in the learning process and language skills training for foreign children (Kim and Pelleriaux, 2004).

- In French primary schools, when pupils have particular learning difficulties they can obtain help through *programmes personalisés d'aide et de progrès* (PPAP). Such programmes are designed in partnership with the parents to suit the pupil, following a diagnosis of particular difficulties. The programme is implemented by the ordinary class teacher who in most situations will not require additional help. Where additional specialist help is required, it is delivered through the *réseaux d'aides spécialisées pour les élèves en difficulté* (RASED) (Ministry of National Education, Higher Education and Research, France, 2004).

There are also interventions designed for those with diagnosed special needs. Special needs can be defined narrowly or quite broadly, as the example from Finland demonstrates. While this report will not tackle special education (examined in OECD 2004a), it has been very important in demonstrating the capacity of school systems to effectively integrate pupils with very diverse learning needs (see also Chapter 6). One report from Austria concludes:

"One of the main reasons for the broad acceptance of integration is that the educational concepts and forms of instruction in these classes are seen by the large majority of parents also as a chance for the pupils without disabilities. Practical experience revealed that initial fears that pupils with special needs would disturb work in class and hamper the progress of the other pupils had been unfounded. Studies proved that successful integration classes are good practice examples characterised by features which benefit both the children with and without special needs. In such classes the individual needs of all pupils get more attention and social learning is stressed more than in conventional classes. The evaluation of integration trials showed that the pupils without special needs assess their relations with the teachers and their personal well-being more positively and that they see better chances of participation in this form of education." (Pechar *et al.*, 2005)

The teaching profession plays the main role in delivering these classroom practices. Teachers need the skills to handle classrooms which are increasingly diverse in terms of attainment, social and ethnic background. This increasing diversity in the classroom flows from school reform – comprehensive schooling and reductions in tracking and streaming – and social change, including rising rates of international migration. Developing the skills involved requires professional development. Chapter 5, under the heading of resources, discusses how the key resource of teachers can be used to help those with the greatest needs, and Chapter 6 examines this issue in relation to teaching migrants and minorities.

Box 4.3. **The teaching profession in Finland**

Good teaching is central to the success of Finnish schools. There are extensive high status programmes for teachers preparing them to work with children with diverse learning needs in integrated classes.

"Teaching practice is interspersed with classroom practice, in a series of internships – placements with different pedagogical problems – typically one period in each of the four years of preparation, in either a local school or a university-sponsored teacher-training school. One principle of teacher preparation is that experience in the classroom, guided by a mentor-teacher, provides new teachers with the ability to cope with a variety of classroom issues, from students performing at different levels to the special needs of immigrant children to more difficult cases of foetal alcohol syndrome or attention deficit hyperactivity disorder requiring evaluation by special education. Another is that teachers are prepared to become independent professionals, with judgment and expertise in both subject matter and pedagogical alternatives, rather than automatons delivering a teacher-proofed curriculum. As the Ministry of Education explained the purpose of pedagogical studies, 'their aim is to produce teaching professionals who are able to develop their own work and their working community.'"

Source: Grubb *et al.*, 2005.

4.2. Schools reaching out to homes

While the effect of social background on education outcomes is well-established, the mechanisms are less well understood. PISA and other research show that few mediating factors stand out, but one of them is having books at home (see Figure 4.2). Most probably, it is not the availability of books

Figure 4.2. **How home circumstances affect school performance**

Percentage of variance in student performance explained by different factors (2003)

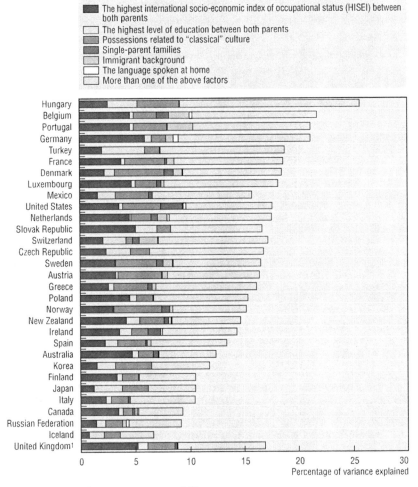

1. Response rate too low to ensure comparability.

Source: OECD (2004b), *Learning for Tomorrow's World: First Results from PISA 2003*, OECD, Paris.

per se which is important but books as an indicator of the social and cultural value in family life.

In support of this viewpoint, there is good evidence that parents' communication with their children and the encouragement they give their learning contribute to learning outcomes. Some disadvantaged children may not get this home support because of other pressures on parents, poor environment for home study, or because some parents may not understand the need to support their children's learning, or lack the ability to engage with the subject matter. This is a challenge for equity.

4.3. Home influence on school performance

Parental support can improve attainment through:

● help or guidance with homework;

● funding of private tuition outside school;

● informal encouragement of learning;

● advice and support in choice of learning options and institutions of study;

● provision of home learning resources, including books and ICT, supported by advice on how to use such resources;

● support for participation in extra-curricular activities with educational benefits.

Research shows that greater parental involvement in education encourages more positive attitudes toward school, improves homework habits, reduces absenteeism and dropout, and enhances academic achievement (OECD, 2004b). The more active forms of parental involvement work best. These include working with children at home, greater communication with school, attending and supporting school activities or tutoring children using material provided by teachers (Cotton and Reed Wikelund, 1989). The PIRLS study (Mullis *et al.*, 2003, Exhibit 4.1) reveals that the parents of children with the best performance in reading (in the fourth grade) engaged in activities such as reading books, telling stories, singing songs and playing word and alphabet games prior to their children's entry to primary school. On average, higher engagement of parents in early home literacy activities improves scores by around 20 points on the PIRLS reading scale. According to Ho and Willms (1996), direct parental involvement in school such as volunteering and attending parent-teacher associations meetings has (unsurprisingly) smaller effects on academic outcomes than helping children with their school work and monitoring time spent watching television or going out on school nights. General support and involvement by parents, such as a display of interest in school programmes and discussing the student's day at school, work best.

Although parents' social class and levels of education are related to educational outcomes, the quality of the home learning environment is the key variable at work (Effective Provision of Pre-School Education Project). Students from minority and disadvantaged backgrounds may be disadvantaged educationally because they lack access to networks of well-educated adults – social capital, both inside and outside of school. If, in addition to providing stronger support for learning, wealthier or better-informed parents also have the ability to obtain better quality schooling for their children, or simply live in areas where schools are better or the peer environment in the schools is more supportive – as is so often the case in practice – the inequitable effect of background on outcomes will be compounded.

Policy measures to link schools with homes

Studies have shown that successful schools foster greater communication with parents, encourage parents to assist their children with school work at home, and recruit parents to work as volunteers or participate in school governance (Epstein, 1995). While this may improve school outcomes, it also presents a dilemma in respect of equity. Untargeted blanket measures to encourage parent-school partnerships will almost inevitably come to fruition more readily in schools where parents are better educated and have more resources. The perverse effect might be to improve outcomes but only in schools in better-off areas – thereby increasing inequity. For that reason, initiatives need to reach out to the most disadvantaged parts of society. Relevant measures include supporting homework (either at home or at school), strengthening communication channels between parents and schools and helping to develop learning communities.

Supporting homework

On average across the OECD, time spent out of school either doing homework, working with a tutor or other types of courses of out-of-school study makes up more than 20% of total learning time, but in some countries the figure is as much as 40% (See Figure 4.3).

There has been a growing debate over the length of homework assignments (see, for example, Brown Center Report on American Education, 2003). Proponents argue that homework supports school learning, creates a link between parents and school, and encourages and develops habits of independent study. Betts (1997), looking at US students in grades 7 to 12, found time spent on mathematics homework to be a stronger driver of achievement than any of the standard measures of school quality, such as teacher education and experience or class size. Critics argue that too much homework creates inequity, displaces other valuable activities such as sport, music, play and social interaction and causes conflict between parents and children.

Many immigrant and disadvantaged parents are not able to help their children with their homework, either because of weak skills in the relevant language or lack of time. Nor can they afford to pay someone to help their children keep up with their classmates. In response, one approach is to reach out to parents to inform them of the importance of homework, strengthen communication (using interpreters in immigrant communities) and provide assistance to parents so that they can help their children. Schools can also

Figure 4.3. **Learning time in and out of school (2003)**

In number of hours

Students' reports of the average number of hours spent on the following "out-of-school" activities during each school week:

■ Homework or other study set by their teachers
▨ Working with a tutor
▢ Attending out-of-school classes
▢ Other study

Students' reports of the average number of hours spent on the following "in-school" activities during each school week:

■ Instructional time
▨ Remedial classes
▢ Enrichment classes

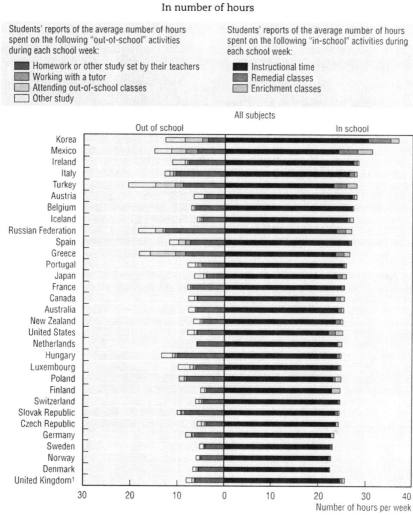

1. Response rate too low to ensure comparability.

Source: OECD (2004b), *Learning for Tomorrow's World: First Results from PISA 2003*, OECD, Paris.

provide additional time for children who need homework support on school premises.

In Ireland, a school completion programme to help youth at risk includes a strategy of before-school and after-school support, delivered outside school hours. These services, delivered in partnership with other agencies, assist the personal and social development of young people and also support parents. Activities include:

- *Clubs*: Homework clubs (with food), computer and music clubs.
- *Programmes and Projects*: Drugs education, family therapy, mentoring programmes, community development.
- *Parental support*: Parenting courses, ICT skills, providing support for children's homework (Exchange House Travellers Service).

Strengthening communication with parents

While some countries have formal arrangements to link parents and schools, these may not work for disadvantaged groups, because of linguistic obstacles, lack of time, conflicting work schedules, lack of confidence, or because the parents involved see education as either the school's exclusive job or simply unimportant. PIRLS (Mullis *et al.*, 2003, p.238) shows that in the majority of countries, better cooperation between the school and home is associated with higher attainment. In Canada, France, the Netherlands, New Zealand and the United States, contacts between parents and school are frequent according to school heads. More than 50% of schools say that they maintain close relationships with the majority of parents. These contacts are less common in the Czech Republic, Hungary, Norway, the Slovak Republic, Slovenia, Sweden and Turkey, where less than 35% of schools say that they are often in touch with parents. According to PISA data, the influence of parent groups on decision making at school tends to be strongest in the areas of instructional content and assessment practices, weaker in budgeting and weakest in the area of staffing.

In most education systems, communication arrangements are locally determined. In Norway, recent government initiatives (Report No. 30 to the *Storting* [2003-2004]) recognised the importance of family-school relationships and sought to clarify the division of responsibility between homes, schools and teachers. But it also underlined that all three groups share the responsibility of communicating regarding the education of each child (Ministry of Education and Research, Norway).

Setting national priorities is vital, but it has to be followed up by effective practices. Different communication channels can be used. In addition to the traditional report card and newsletters, tools such as DVDs, which show the school at work, can be effective. For children of parents who are less familiar with the working of schools, the achievements of children need to be relayed to parents and communication needs to be balanced. If the only information to reach home is bad news, there is little chance of winning support from the family for the efforts being made at school. The communication style also needs to be suited to the nature of the community. Telephone calls to workers during normal business hours might not be answered; letters sent home may not be read or understood.

In Sweden for example, in a school where there was a high concentration of immigrant students, the school *Sunnadals Hela Världans Skolan* collaborated with local organisations (such as the National Naval Museum, the music club, the athletics club) to create links with the local community. A cafe and meeting centre have been set up in the main hall of the school, which can be used by the neighbourhood for their activities, and where study circles for adults are organised in the evenings, with support from the municipality

---

Box 4.4. **Developing learning communities**

- In Ireland, the Schools' Business Partnership (SBP) matches up individual schools participating in the School Completion Programme with a local company. A teacher seconded through the Department of Education and Science acts as Education Programme Executive with the SBP. Programmes include the Student Mentoring Programme, a two-year programme for 16-to-18-year-olds where employees from the company mentor students. To date, 500 corporate volunteers from 16 companies and their partnering schools have participated. It is claimed that this programme has resulted in a number of additional students continuing on to third level (OECD, 2005i).

- In Barcelona, the City Educational Project (PEC) brings together representatives of civil society and public institutions to promote an integrated education network. Projects range from renovating school gardens to the establishment of an education and immigration forum. The Barcelona Educational Coordination Board (1991) brings together organisations that offer educational activities for schoolchildren. Activities include music, museums, films and art, public transport, and science and technology (Institut d'Educació, Ayuntament de Barcelona, 2004).

- *Fryshuset*, a Swedish youth centre created in 1984 by the YMCA, is now "owned" by young people and the local community. The centre runs cultural and sports activities and innovative social projects to prevent violence and promote social (re-)integration in a multicultural urban environment. These include the *Shadaf Heroes*, a movement of Muslim boys opposing violence to girls in their community; *Exit*, assisting youngsters to leave the neo-nazi movement; and *Calm Street*, a group of unemployed young people hired to patrol and prevent violence in the public transport sector. *Calm Street* also offers training in conflict resolution, first aid, law and ethics etc. to juniors. *The Knowledge Centre*, an upper secondary school combining sports and cultural education with the core curriculum of the gymnasium, is the educational pillar of Fryshuset. The school has 850 students (Nicaise *et al.*, 2005).

(parenting courses, intercultural evenings, meetings with employers and the unemployment office etc.). One other school organised informal meetings with tutors or community mediators who could speak the language of the community in which the school was located. Free coffee and small gatherings took place once a week for those who wanted to approach the schools. Additionally, a local person was hired to approach families, help them with their questions and try to bring the school closer to their families. Another school hired interpreters for parent meetings (Nicaise *et al.*, 2005).

Creating learning communities

One view of education is that learning depends heavily on a range of actors in a "learning community" and not just on the teacher and the school. In this model, parents are indispensable partners in the education of their children, rather than customers in a competitive market. Parents can help teachers understand the behaviour and needs of their children and make teaching more effective. They also contribute with their own diverse skills, which are often valuable complements to those of teachers. In exchange, the role of the school is defined as a resource centre for the development of the local community, which means that it gives all stakeholders, including parents, a sense of ownership and aims to respond in a flexible way to their needs.

Employers also play an important role, for example by permitting their workers to visit their children's school when necessary during working hours. Education authorities could encourage employer support for working parents through awards for community development or possibly through tax relief for firms which provide verified employer support over a designated period of time.

4.4. Summary conclusions and recommendations

Step 5: Identify and provide systematic help to those who fall behind at school and reduce high rates of school-year repetition

Evidence

- In some school systems, up to one-quarter of students repeat a year at some point. In others it is rare. Some countries, such as Luxembourg, are taking steps to reduce the extent of repetition.
- Although year repetition is often popular with teachers, there is little evidence that children gain benefit from it. Repetition is expensive – the full economic cost is up to USD 20 000 equivalent for each student who repeats a year – but schools have few incentives to take into account the costs involved.
- The classroom is the first level of intervention for equity. Evidence shows that it is possible to improve classroom attainment with methods such as

formative assessment – a process of feeding back information about performance to student and teacher and adapting and improving teaching and learning in response, particularly with students at risk.

- "Reading Recovery" strategies – short-term, intensive interventions of one-on-one lessons – can help many poor readers to catch up.

- Finland uses a hierarchy of successive formal and informal interventions to assist those falling behind at school. This approach appears to be successful: only 1% of 15-year-olds are unable to demonstrate basic functional reading skills, while the OECD average is 7%.

Policy recommendations

- *High rates of year repetition in some countries need to be reduced* by changing incentives for schools and encouraging alternative approaches.

- *Interventions in the classroom can be very effective in tackling underachievement.* Among the approaches available, we can highlight formative assessment, reading recovery strategies and careful monitoring.

- Many countries could usefully follow *the successful Finnish approach to learning difficulties,* offering a sequence of intensifying interventions which draw back into the mainstream those who fall behind.

- *Teaching professionals should receive support to develop their in-classroom techniques* to help those in the class who are falling behind.

Step 6: Strengthen the links between school and home to help disadvantaged parents help their children to learn

Student learning benefits from an effective school-home relationship, but children from deprived backgrounds may not benefit from this advantage because of weak support at home.

Evidence

- On average, children in OECD countries spend more than 20% of their total learning time out of school – doing homework, working with a tutor or on other activities.

- Home factors, including parental support for education, engagement with children's learning and cultural assets (like books), are associated with stronger school performance.

- Homework can improve school outcomes, but reliance on homework may also threaten equity, since some children lack the home support necessary to realise its benefits.

- Parental involvement – working with children at home and actively participating in school activities – does improve results. All other things being equal, schools that foster communication and participation by parents, and encourage and assist parents to support their children with their school work tend to have better outcomes.

Policy recommendations

● To support learning among disadvantaged children, schools need to target their efforts to *improve communication with parents* in the most disadvantaged homes and help develop environments conducive to learning.

● *After-school homework clubs* at school may also provide an environment that supports homework for those with weak home support.

References

Betts, J. (1997), "The Two-Legged Stool: The Neglected Role of Educational Standards in Improving America's Public Schools", *Working Paper 97-32*, University of California, Department of Economics, San Diego.

Black, P. and D. William (1998), "Assessment and Classroom Learning", in *Assessment in Education*, Vol. 5, No. 1, March 1998, p. 140.

Brooks, G. (2002), "What Works for Children with Literacy Difficulties: The Effectiveness of Intervention Schemes", Department for Education and Skills (DfES) report 380.31, DfES, London.

Brown Center Report on American Education (2003), "How Well Are American Students Learning? With Special Section on Homework, Charter Schools, and Rural School Achievement", Vol. 1, No. 4, Brookings Institution, Washington, DC.

Burroughs-Lange, S. (n.d.), *Evaluation of Reading Recovery in London Schools: Every Child A Reader 2005-2006*, Institute of Education, University of London, London.

Coradi Vellacott, M. and S. Wolter (2004), *Equity in the Swiss Education System: Dimensions, Causes and Policy Responses. National Report from Switzerland contributing to the OECD's Review of Equity in Education*, Swiss Coordination Center for Research in Education.

Cotton, K. and K. Reed Wikelund (1989), *Student and Parent Involvement in Education*, retrieved March, 2006, School Improvement Research Series, Northwest Regional Educational Laboratory, *www.nwrel.org/scpd/sirs/3/cu6.html*.

Dalton, M., P. Ferguson and S. Jimerson (2001), "Sorting out of Successful Failures: Exploratory Analyses of Factors Associated with Academic and Behavioural Outcomes of Retained Students", *Psychology in the Schools*, Vol. 38(4), John Wiley and Sons, Inc.

Effective Provision of Pre-School Education project, *www.ioe.ac.uk/schools/ecpe/eppe/index.htm*.

Epstein, J. (1995), "School/family/community Partnerships: Caring for the Children we Share", *Phi Delta Kappa*, 76(9), pp. 701-712.

Eurydice, *The Information Network on Education in Europe*, *www.eurydice.org/Eurybase/frameset_eurybase.html*.

Exchange House Travellers Service, *www.exchangehouse.ie/afterschools.htm*.

Flere, S. (2004), *Educational Equity and Inequity in Slovenia: Country Analytical Report.*

Grubb N., S. Field, H. Marit Jahr and J. Neumüller (2005), *Equity in Education Thematic Review: Finland Country Note*, OECD, Paris, *www.oecd.org/dataoecd/49/40/36376641.pdf.*

Haut Conseil de l'Évaluation de l'École (2004), Avis 14.

Ho Sui-Chu, E. and J. Willms (1996), "Effects of Parental Iinvolvement on Eighth-Grade Achievement", *Sociology of Education,* 69(2), pp. 126-141.

Hoffman, N., M.L. Ferreira, S. Field and B. Levin (2005), *Equity in Education Thematic Review: Hungary Country Note*, OECD, Paris.

Institut d'Educació, Ayuntament de Barcelona (2004), PEC 2004-2007, Barcelona Educational Coordination Board (2005), Schools and Civic Entities: Networking Schools.

Jimerson, S., E. Carlson, M. Rotert, B. Egeland and L. Sroufe (1997), "A Prospective, Longitudinal Study of the Correlates and Consequences of Early Grade Retention", *Journal of School Psychology*, Vol. 35, No. 1, Pergamon/Elsevier, pp. 3-25.

Kim, T. and K. Pelleriaux (2004), *Equity in the Flemish Educational System: Country Analytical Report*, University of Antwerp.

Luxembourg, ministère de l'Éducation nationale et de la Formation professionnelle, 2005, Analyse des "Klassenwiderholens" im primaren und postprimaren Bereich, *www.gouvernement.lu/salle_presse/actualite/2005/09/28delvaux/etude_redoublement.pdf.*

Lycée de l'Essouriau (2005), "*La première de détermination S-ES du lycée de l'Essouriau*", Lycée de l'Essouriau, Les Ulis, *www.innovation-pedagogique.ac-versailles.fr/IMG/pdf/05-06-lgtl_Essouriau-Les_Ulis.pdf.*

Ministry of National Education, Higher Education and Research, France (2004), *L'équité dans l'éducation en France: Rapport de base national présenté dans le cadre de l'activité de l'OCDE*, Paris.

Ministry of Education and Research, Norway, *www.odin.dep.no/ufd.*

Mortimore, P., S. Field. and B. Pont (2005), *Equity in Education Thematic Review: Norway Country Note*, OECD, Paris, *www.oecd.org/dataoecd/10/6/35892523.pdf.*

Mullis, I., M. Martin, E. Gonzalez and A. Kennedy (2003), *PIRLS 2001 International Report: IEA's Study of Reading Literacy Achievement in Primary Schools in 35 Countries*, International Study Center, Lynch School of Education, Boston College.

Nicaise, I., G. Esping-Andersen, B. Pont and P. Tunstall (2005), *Equity in Education Thematic Review: Sweden Country Note*, OECD, Paris, *www.oecd.org/dataoecd/10/5/35892546.pdf.*

OECD (2004a), *Equity in Education: Students with Disabilities, Learning Difficulties and Disadvantages*, OECD, Paris.

OECD (2004b), *Learning for Tomorrow's World: First Results from PISA 2003*, OECD, Paris.

OECD (2005c), *Education at a Glance: OECD Indicators 2005*, OECD, Paris.

OECD (2005h), *Formative Assessment: Improving Learning in Secondary Classrooms*, OECD, Paris.

OECD (2005i), *Promoting Partnership for Inclusion: Country Report National System Policies and Practices Concerning Children and Youth at Risk – Ireland*, OECD, CERI, Paris.

OECD, "England Case Study Visit, Innovative Approaches to School Leadership", OECD, Paris, available at *www.oecd.org/edu/schoolleadership.* Paul, J.-J. (1997), " Le redoublement à l'école : une maladie universelle? ", *International Review of Education*, 43(5-6), pp. 611-627, forthcoming.

Paul, J.-J. and T. Troncin (2004), "Les apports de la recherche sur l'impact du redoublement comme moyen de traiter les difficultés scolaires au cours de la scolarité obligatoire", Haut Conseil de l'Évaluation de l'École, No. 14.

Pechar, H., M. Unger and M. Bonisch (2005), *Equity in Education: An Inventory of the Situation in Austria*, unpublished, Vienna.

Reading Recovery Council of North America, *www.readingrecovery.org*.

Swiss Contribution to Eurybase – the Information Database on Education Systems in Europe (2001), Information Documentation Éducation Suisse, Berne, *www.edk.ch/PDF_Downloads/Bildungswesen_CH/Eurydice_00e.pdf*.

Teese, R., P. Aasen, S. Field and B. Pont (2005), *Equity in Education Thematic Review: Spain Country Note*, OECD, Paris, *www.oecd.org/dataoecd/41/39/36361409.pdf*.

Willms, J.D. (2003), *Student Engagement at School: A Sense of Belonging and Participation, Results from PISA 2000*, OECD, Paris.

ISBN 978-92-64-03259-0
No More Failures: Ten Steps to Equity in Education
© OECD 2007

Chapter 5

Resources and Outcomes

This chapter looks at the way in which resources are distributed in educational systems and how outcome measures are used to direct the system; both have profound implications for equity. It examines the vertical allocation of resources between different educational levels, and argues that early childhood education and care and basic education are equity priorities. It looks at horizontal allocation across institutions and regions, explores the merits of different approaches to targeting resources for schools and individuals who need additional help, and examines ways of compensating for regional inequalities. The chapter then examines two key ways in which outcome measures can be used for policy purposes. It examines the use of numerically defined policy targets for equity, discussing their potential pitfalls as well as their merits. It also explores the issue of schools testing, its implications for equity, pros and cons of publication at school level and support measures necessary for schools identified as underperforming.

One of the biggest challenges faced by education ministers is how to deal with competing demands for spending – to renovate schools, expand universities for increasing student numbers, find additional funds to pay teachers wages or target support to those with learning difficulties.

Frequently, the question of priorities is avoided. This is partly because budgets for different sectors are often looked at separately, and it is much easier to see that schools need repairs than to fund those repairs by closing kindergartens, or increasing taxes. Sometimes the budget challenge is shared with other ministries – budgets for adult learning often fall to employment ministries, while ministries for social affairs sometime take responsibility for early childhood education and care and ministries of science for parts of tertiary education. Inevitably, competition between ministries for resources makes it harder to agree on any strategic view of priorities. Even when responsibilities are clear, it is sometimes easier to avoid the issue. Clear, well-thought-out priorities are the mark of strong education policy. But not everything can be a priority, and no one wants to give that message to a non-priority sector.

This chapter looks at priorities for equity and links that discussion to targets and outcomes. Policy targets – either national or local – are a concrete way of demonstrating not just that something is desirable, but that steps are being taken to realise that end.

5.1. Allocating resources across educational sectors

Priorities and resources

The main criterion of a priority is a willingness to commit valued resources to the desired objective. That does not just mean money. Political capital – willingness to bear political risks – costs nothing in pure financial terms. No major reform is without determined opponents and sometimes the most sorely needed reforms make the most enemies. In a democracy, some unpopular reforms are possible, but governments seeking re-election will limit their extent and number. This means being very clear about priorities.

When money is involved, the function of priority setting across sectors is to determine the allocation of resources at the margin. If, for example, primary education is identified as a greater priority than secondary education, it means that any additional resources are directed to primary schools, or, if there are budgetary cuts, they are concentrated on secondary schools. In the longer term, year-on-year adjustment of budgets in one direction or another represents a clear statement of priorities. A great deal of priority setting will remain implicit, not least because of the political difficulty in saying that a particular sector is not a priority.

Chapter 2 described how the general expansion of education has not delivered as much equity as some hoped. Further increases in aggregate expenditure on education may not yield equity benefits. This adds force to the argument that additional education expenditure should be targeted at the education sectors which are most conducive to equity.

There are some exceptions. In Russia, general increases in public spending on education would be very helpful, as they could alleviate some of the severe inequities associated with current underfunding. While public education at pre-primary, primary and secondary level is free, public spending on education was halved between 1991 and 1999. Over this period, spending per child decreased by 40% in primary and secondary schools and by 70% in higher education. About a third of schools need urgent major repairs and a quarter of primary and secondary schools have no running water. Only 59% have proper sewage systems. This has led to a parallel system based on widespread informal payments for education in which parents typically pay for teaching materials, redecoration, guarding of the premises and trips. This is also the case for tertiary education, which includes official payments for books, entrance and examination fees, and unofficial payments including tutoring fees, entrance bribes or pseudo tutorship, and payment for course work. This inevitably discriminates against low income families (Ministry of Education, Russian Federation, 2005).

Evidence of sectoral priorities

In most OECD countries, annual tuition expenditure per student increases with age, growing gradually from pre-primary to tertiary level. The increase is partly attributable to smaller class sizes in secondary school, and partly to higher salaries for teachers in later stages of the system. The question these differences raise is fundamental. Are they justified? Or do they reflect historical accident, or the relative bargaining power of high status secondary and tertiary teaching personnel relative to primary school teachers?

The argument is partly one of efficiency, of deciding how to spread tuition expenditure, and therefore one of effort – over the entire period of learning so as to maximise learning outcomes. For example, does one get a better result from putting more resources into primary schools or secondary schools? But it is also partly a question about equity, since not all students obtain the benefits of early childhood or post-compulsory education. Setting aside longer time

Figure 5.1. **Spending rises as students progress (2003)**

Public and private expenditure per student in OECD countries, in full-time equivalents (estimation)

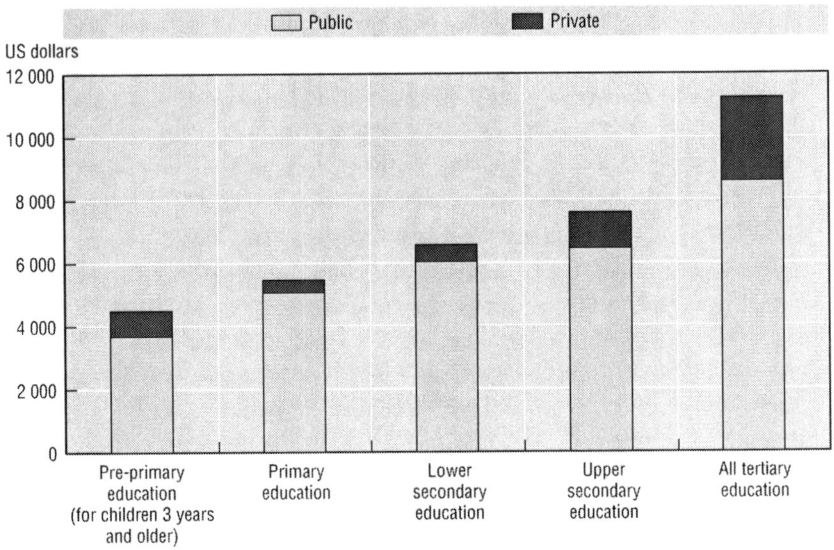

Source: OECD Education database.

trends, we have evidence of expenditure shifts over the last decade which reveal something of the current sectoral priorities of countries.

Some shifts in expenditure between sectors are attributable to demographic pressures. For example, if there are more young adults and fewer children, it would be natural to spend more on universities and less on schools. Arguably, expenditure per student tells a clearer story.

Figure 5.2 shows that priorities in some countries are shifting markedly between tertiary education and other sectors. In many countries, there have been large increases in the number of students in tertiary education – over 50% in the Czech Republic, Greece, Hungary, Korea, Poland and the Slovak Republic. Some countries – for example Greece, Hungary and Mexico – have matched the numerical increase with growing expenditure on tertiary education. Others have contained the pressure by reducing per capita expenditure on tertiary education as numbers have grown. (These data include both public and private expenditure – so they do not show, for example, whether countries are shifting the burden of tertiary education expenditure to the private sector.)

Household expenditure on education

Private households commonly contribute to the costs of education, through fees, learning materials such as textbooks and the maintenance of

Figure 5.2. **Universities or schools? Funding priorities**
Indices of change in real expenditure and numbers of students in 2003 (1995 = 100)

☐ Real expenditure at primary, secondary and post-secondary non-tertiary level
■ Real expenditure at tertiary level
◇ The number of students at primary, secondary and post-secondary non-tertiary level
▲ The number of students at tertiary level

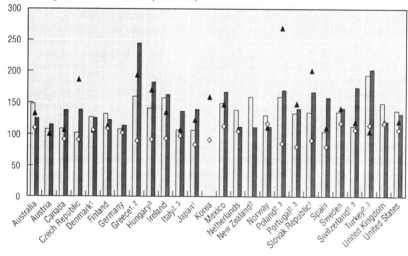

1. Some levels of education are included with others.
2. Public expenditure only.
3. Public institutions only.
Source: OECD (2006c), *Education at a Glance: OECD Indicators 2006*, OECD, Paris.

students during education. In OECD countries, this spending is significant (OECD 2006c, Tables B3.2a and B3.2b), especially in early childhood and tertiary education and relatively, it bears heavily on less advantaged families.* Comparing countries, the burden depends heavily on the generosity of the state in matters such as school meals, books and other school materials, and transportation to school. While compulsory education is mainly free, there are wide variations in payments for teaching materials and grants for school-age children. Table 5.1 sets out the main characteristics of funding in selected OECD countries.

It is striking that some countries tie grants for disadvantaged children to school performance. While in theory this might encourage school performance, it could also promote dropout, since it penalises those whose

---

* The OECD data do not include private funding outside educational institutions such as, for example, private tutoring. Thus the family expenditure on education may be even much higher in some cases.

115

Table 5.1. Public financial support for students in compulsory and post-compulsory school (without tertiary)

Direct support	Indirect support
Belgium (Flanders): Scholarship for full-time secondary students from low-income families of Belgian nationality.	Free school materials (*e.g.* exercise and text books).
Finland: Grants and loans available for full-time post-comprehensive studies (at least eight weeks at upper secondary schools, folk high school and vocational schools). Amount depends on type of school, age and marital status of the student, and type of accommodation.	In primary school: Free learning materials, hot meals at school, health and dental care and, if necessary, transport and accommodation. In upper secondary schools or vocational institutions: free meals and student welfare services. Some financial aid for school travel available.
France: An allowance for low-income families with children aged 6 to 18 enrolled in school. In lower secondary school: grants for students from poor background, with premiums for completion for progression and good performance. Secondary schools have a fund for disadvantaged students.	Basic school books are free. At upper secondary level, books are not free but many regions provide students with free materials or with financial aid to buy them.
Hungary: A general monthly subsidy for parents of children below the age of 18 or students in full-time secondary education up to the age of 22.	Free textbooks and meals at school for disadvantaged pupils in full-time school education.
Norway: Financial support from the State Educational Loan Fund for students and apprentices from low-income families. The student loans are interest free during the studies. A child allowance for each child until the age of 16.	In primary and secondary education, learning materials, health and dental care and transport are free, if needed.
Russian Federation:	Different forms of support such as free meals and textbooks. In practice support is limited. In 2003, the federal government ceased funding school meals from the central budget. This means that only wealthier regions can maintain reasonable standards.
Slovenia: Scholarship for secondary school students calculated on the basis of the student's family income, the location of study or residence during study, the year of study and study results.	In elementary school: transportation for children living more than four kilometres from their school. One meal in school per day for disadvantaged students in primary and upper secondary school.
Spain: A grant or a loan for upper secondary students, granted on the basis of family income and academic performance (for example, grants are not given to students who are repeating a year).	In compulsory schooling: the costs of meals, transport and boarding for disadvantaged children.
Sweden: A child allowance for each child until they reach 16 years of age. Grant to cover living costs and other expenses for upper secondary students.	In compulsory education and to some extent in upper secondary education: free books, meals and transportation to the nearest school.
Switzerland: In most cantons, child allowance for a child to the age of 16. If the child remains in education, most cantons continue to provide child allowance payments until the child reaches 25.	
United Kingdom: Educational Maintenance Allowance (EMA) a payment to students aged 16 to 18 from low income families in full-time education. Evaluation shows that EMA increases retention by between 4 and 8%, with especially strong effects on those from poor backgrounds and with low prior academic achievement. Many of the students are displaced from economic inactivity into education. Similar measures have been introduced in Australia and Mexico.	

Source: Crouch, D., "School meals around the world", 30 March 2005, Guardian Unlimited; Dearden, L., *et al.* (2006), *Education Subsidies and School Drop-Out Rates, Center for the Economics of Education*, London School of Economics; Eurydice; The Swiss Portal, *www.ch.ch*; and reports prepared for the Equity in Education Thematic Review (available at *www.oecd.org/edu/equity/equityineducation*).

commitment to school is most questionable. There is evidence, for example from the UK educational maintenance allowance scheme, that grants may improve retention among disadvantaged students (Dearden *et al.*, 2006). It is therefore potentially damaging to equity to withdraw them for children at risk. But some basic conditions do make sense. In Mexico, *Oportunidades* grants targeted to poor families are conditional. Transfer of cash grants depends on children staying at school and undertaking regular health checks (OECD, 2005b).

The claims of each sector

Spending money on one part of the education system has implications for other parts, since individual students move from one stage to the next. Younger people staying on at school implies more applicants at tertiary level. One difficult challenge for any educational system is to develop a systemic viewpoint and link it to decisions about sectoral priorities. For example it makes little sense to have an exceptional primary school system if the outcomes are wasted in weak secondary schools (see also Cunha *et al.*, 2005). As well as just planning numbers and forecasting their flow through the system, this requires some attention to the quality of outcomes and consistency across successive stages of the educational system.

Early childhood education and care

There is extensive evidence that an environment which is healthy, caring, and educative for very young children yields large positive returns over a lifetime, particularly for the most disadvantaged (McCabe and Smyth, 2000; Carneiro and Heckman, 2003; Heckman, 1999; Leseman, 2002; OECD, 2006d). In the United States, for example, the Perry Preschool experiment, the Abecedarian Project and the Chicago Child-Parent Center Program have shown that children from disadvantaged backgrounds who receive good quality early childhood education and care (ECEC) have better school outcomes and are less likely to become involved in crime. In France, Sweden and the United Kingdom, additional studies show that participation in high quality early childhood education and care is positively associated with long-term cognitive, social and emotional development of children, with school readiness and school performance, and has especially strong associations for those with disadvantaged backgrounds (Goodman and Sianesi, 2005). Sylva *et al.* (2003) found that the more extensive systems of preschool education in terms of enrolment and duration significantly increase equality of opportunity, as measured by a lower dependence of eighth-grade students' test scores on their family background.

Figure 5.3 shows the long-term outcomes from the US Perry Program, directed at extremely disadvantaged American children. It compares

Figure 5.3. **Starting strong: big returns from early childhood education**

The Perry Preschool study: the impact of early childhood education
and care as measured in two randomised samples

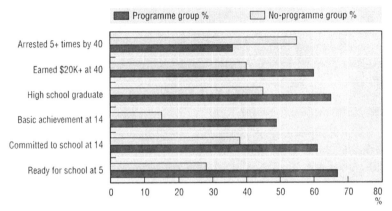

Source: OECD (2006d), *Starting Strong II: Early Childhood Education and Care*, OECD, Paris, Figure 5.1.

outcomes for treatment and control groups in a fully randomised controlled trial. Each dollar invested in preschool repaid itself nearly 13 times over through earnings benefits arising from more high school completions, better labour market experience and reduced social costs in areas such as crime. Barnett concludes that the national cost of failing to provide at least two years of quality ECEC is extremely high, of the order of USD 100 000 for each child born into poverty (Barnett, 1995). While this evidence relates to interventions undertaken a number of years ago with a heavily disadvantaged group, and the same returns could not be expected from any more general intervention, much weaker returns would still be very attractive to public policy makers.

As explained in Chapter 2, education is a dynamic process, in which general cognitive and social skills, acquired early, provide the basis for further learning. This means that for those who fail to learn early on it is hard to catch up later in life (Carneiro and Heckman, 2003; Cunha *et al.*, 2005; Heckman, 1999). This evidence is in striking contrast to the tendency of education systems across the OECD, illustrated in the *per capita* expenditure figures, to intensify education investment as children get older. While there may be justifiable reasons for the pattern, it may also require further scrutiny.

Historically, ECEC was often considered simply a method for taking care of children when their parents were at work. Now, it is better recognised as a crucial stage of education with large long-term benefits, both in cognitive and social skills; and the right to ECEC has very often been detached from the employment situation of parents. For example, Sweden has recently removed the restriction on access to ECEC for parents who are unemployed or on parental leave.

NO MORE FAILURES: TEN STEPS TO EQUITY IN EDUCATION – ISBN 978-92-64-03259-0 – © OECD

There are large variations between countries in government support for and participation in ECEC. Many OECD countries have already introduced free-of-charge ECEC at least for all disadvantaged children. For example, in Belgium, all children from the age of two-and-a-half and in France all children from the age of three have a right to free ECEC. Sweden, where free ECEC is provided to all four-year-old and five-year-old children, has introduced free half-day provision for bilingual children from the age of three. In systems where ECEC is not free of charge, research suggests that family income is one of the predictors of enrolment in early education and care programmes, which may be particularly relevant to immigrants and minorities (Chiswick and DebBurnam, 2004; Bainbridge et al., 2005). But badly designed public support to families may provide parents with more financial incentives to keep their children at home than to send them to ECEC. In Norway, parents of young children who make very limited or no use of pre-primary provision and subsidised day care have received a cash transfer (the cash benefit scheme). The aim of this initiative was to provide parents with a wider range of choice of care for their children and to distribute public transfers equally among families regardless of the childcare arrangement made by parents. One of effects of the cash benefit scheme might be the lower participation rate of children of immigrant background in ECEC as this financial incentive has more weight (relative to other sources of income) in poorer households (Mortimore et al., 2005). Parents of young children (1-to-2 years) still receive a cash transfer.

Compulsory education

By definition, compulsory education is for all, including weak performers, those who come from disadvantaged social backgrounds or are otherwise at risk. By contrast, even when valiant efforts are made to enhance access, most non-compulsory sectors of education tend to leave out disadvantaged groups. In many OECD countries there is a renewed emphasis on the compulsory phase of education, linked to concerns about standards and quality. Resource pressures may be substantial, particularly in the context of the need to attract and retain good teachers. While there is little evidence that smaller classes or higher teacher pay improves outcomes overall, research shows that well targeted efforts to help struggling learners can help (Rouse, 2000; Hanushek et al., 1998; Hanushek et al., 2001; Levacic and Vignoles, 2000). For these reasons, the compulsory phase of education has a strong prior claim as an equity priority. This is a simple point, but it is nevertheless compelling. Despite this, across OECD countries less than half of all public educational expenditure goes to primary and lower secondary education (approximating to the compulsory phase). One reason for this is that per capita expenditure is higher at upper secondary and tertiary levels (see Figure 5.4).

Figure 5.4. **Where education spending goes (2003)**

Distribution of total public expenditure on education in OECD countries (estimation)

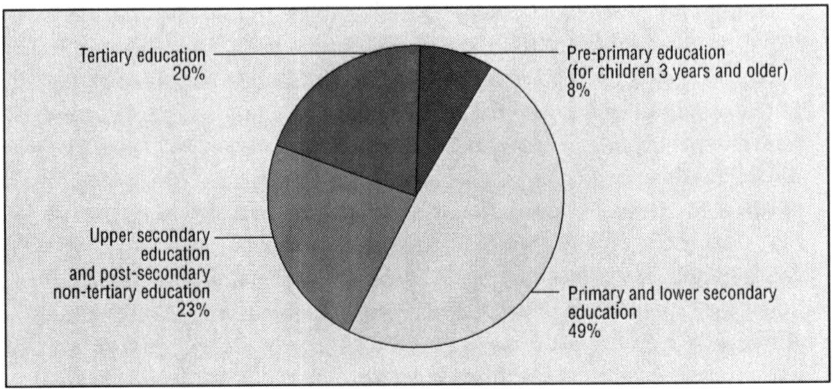

Source: OECD Education database.

Post-compulsory education and adult learning

Outside compulsory education, additional resources are often sought to increase participation – an investment whose outcomes depend on the target group of additional participants. In many OECD countries, upper secondary participation rates have reached 70-80%. At this point, strong equity arguments emerge for increasing participation rates towards 100%, since the remaining 20-30% of the cohort will, almost by definition, be those most likely to be at risk in the labour market.

Adult learning is in a different category, in the face of extensive evidence that those with existing qualifications tend to make the most use of opportunities provided. The challenge in adult learning is to target public investment at those most in need. This is a particular challenge, given that take-up among this group is particularly low. For others, it may be more appropriate to share the costs of adult learning – in line with the benefits – between students, government and employers.

While it may be more cost-effective to give priority to early learning, an additional argument supports the provision of adult learning – that of intergenerational equity. Educational expectations have increased so that older cohorts will not have had the same opportunities as younger cohorts, for example to obtain post-compulsory qualifications. Fairness between generations means that adults who have missed out on initial formal education deserve a reasonable second chance.

Tertiary education

As indicated earlier, substantial increases in overall participation in tertiary education have not generally equalised life chances for those from different backgrounds. On average in OECD countries, around a third of young people (aged 25 to 34) now have tertiary qualifications, but in only two countries (Canada and Japan) does the figure exceed one-half by a small margin. In most OECD countries, tertiary education has not yet reached the point of targeting 100% of the population. Additional participation in tertiary education will therefore in most cases benefit an intermediate group in terms of prior qualifications and attainment. In equity terms, the case for spending public money simply to increase participation is therefore weak. But this should not preclude rethinking priorities in tertiary education. In France for example, 30% of the total budget for tertiary education is spent on the *grandes écoles* and their *classes préparatoires*, a sector which accommodates only about 3% of all tertiary students (Renaut, 2002).

At the same time, an intensive debate has emerged about fees and tertiary education. The equity argument for fees is that subsidies to tertiary tuition go towards those who typically come from well-off families and will themselves be well-off. There are also well-established mechanisms, such as income-contingent loans and grants for target groups, to reduce the risk that fees will deter students from poor families from entering tertiary education. These arguments are weakened, but not eliminated, in the presence of higher marginal income taxes because such taxes act as a graduate tax. Moreover research suggests that in most OECD countries, current levels of public spending on education provide sufficient financial incentives for individuals to seek post-compulsory qualifications (de la Fuente, 2003; Carneiro and Heckman, 2002; Cameron and Heckman, 1999).

In terms of efficiency, there is no aggregate evidence that tertiary expenditure contributes more to economic growth than other parts of education (de la Fuente, 2003) and, given the option of continued tertiary expansion through increased contributions by students, it is difficult to argue that public expenditure is necessary to sustain a tertiary sector of adequate size. In summary therefore, given the strongly competing demands of other sectors, the claims of tertiary education on public education expenditure are weak on both equity and efficiency grounds.

5.2. Allocating resources across individuals, institutions and regions

The previous section looked at the allocation of resources *vertically*, across different sectors of education. This section looks at allocation *horizontally*, between different individuals, institutions and regions. Equity requires that different resources be devoted to different students because some students have greater needs than others. The two main dimensions of equity – fairness and inclusion – imply two approaches:

- directing more resources to students according to indicators of disadvantage or social need, for example family poverty or immigrant status, addressing *fairness*; and

- giving additional resources to students displaying learning weaknesses, addressing *inclusion*.

These approaches overlap in the sense that help given to those with learning difficulties tends also to reduce the impact of social background on outcomes. These two approaches can be pursued at different levels – at the level of the individual, the school and the area.

Compensating for regional economic inequities

In many countries, resourcing decisions are taken locally and some regions have fewer resources or give less priority to education than others. This may result in regional inequities and unevenness in provision. In Spain, for example, Andalusia spends more than twice as much on education (as a percentage of Andalusian GDP) than Spain as a whole (as a percentage of national GDP). But spending per student remains much lower in Andalusia than average expenditure per student in Spain (Figure 5.5).

One other indicator of the extent to which regional economic inequalities can create inequities comes from the United States, in spending on school building and construction. Figure 5.6 shows that public spending on school construction tends to be higher in areas where the population is better off. Higher costs in affluent areas may be part of the explanation, but inequities are also a potential issue.

Later sections will discuss measures designed to direct more resources to schools in disadvantaged areas, but these data are a reminder that many decentralised education systems direct fewer resources to disadvantaged areas because they have a weaker tax base. Many countries redistribute resources to poor areas, on the grounds of their weaker tax base and greater social need. For example, in England, the central government distributes resources from a deprivation fund to local authorities, taking account of their level of disadvantage. In Sweden, the national government redistributes resources from wealthy to poorer municipalities through a grant. (The discretion of local authorities to use these grants as they wish may lead to inequities. The expert team visiting Sweden recommended the re-introduction of earmarked grants, for example to improve the access of minority children to pre-primary education [Nicaise et al., 2005]). In Norway, earmarked grants targeted at disadvantaged populations cover issues such as

Figure 5.5. **Regional variations in education spending: the example of Spain**

Public expenditure on education (other than universities) in Spain
and in two autonomous communities of Spain, with the highest and lowest spending
on education per student

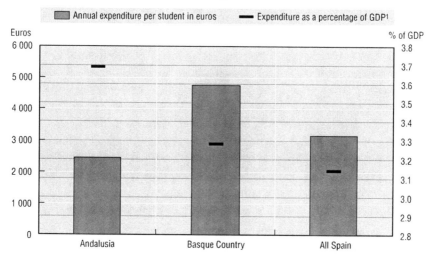

1. In Andalusia and Basque Country, expenditure as a percentage of GDP in the autonomous
communities.

Source: Calero, J. (2005), *Equity in Education Thematic Review: Country Analytical Report – Spain*; Teese, R.,
S. Field, B. Pont (2005), *Equity in Education Thematic Review: Spain Country Note*, OECD, Paris.

Figure 5.6. **Construction spending on public schools in the United States**

Spending across zip code areas divided according to their median household income
(2000)

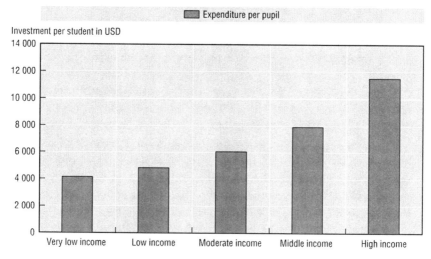

Source: Building Educational Success Together (2006), "Growth and Disparity: A Decade of US Public
School Construction", Building Educational Success Together, Washington, DC.

minority languages, special education, *Saami* education, socio-educational services (Eurydice).

Resources for individual learning weaknesses and disadvantaged areas

Chapter 4 described some ways of tackling individual learning difficulties, including formative assessment, Reading Recovery and the Finnish approach to learning difficulties. In principle, extra resources to support such approaches might be directed to schools where attainment is weak. One rationale is that peer-group effects are important, so that the whole school requires extra help in the face of such clustering. But this approach has a serious downside: poor schools will be rewarded with extra resources while improving schools will be punished by their removal (Demeuse, 2003).

Alternatively, resources can be directed to schools which draw pupils from disadvantaged backgrounds or where the pupils speak a different language at home. There are three potential merits in this approach:

- it avoids the disincentive effect which would flow from giving more resources to schools with poor results;
- it addresses the fairness dimension of equity – seeking to overcome the social background obstacles to educational success;
- it reduces the tendency of school choice regimes to concentrate students from poor social backgrounds in particular schools, since popular schools will be rewarded financially by accepting disadvantaged students.

Recent research reviews show that while effective teaching is particularly helpful for lower performers, they are often least likely to receive it (OECD, 2005j; Darling-Hammond, 2000). In France and the United States, better qualified teachers are less likely to teach in schools containing minority and disadvantaged children (OECD, 2005j; Haycock and Peske, 2004; Hanushek *et al.*, 2001). As mentioned in Chapter 3, social polarisation of schools creates a risk that teacher preferences may direct better teachers to middle class schools. This has been the experience with the French *zones d'éducation prioritaire* (ZEP) (OECD, 2005j; Haycock and Peske, 2006; see also Chapter 4).

In some countries, this problem has been avoided simply because differences between schools are small. In France, attempts are made to attract teachers to schools with disadvantaged intakes through special payments, but Hanushek *et al.* (2001) estimate on the basis of Texas data that schools with disadvantaged, Black or Hispanic students may need to pay 20% or even 50% more in salary than schools with white and Asian children to prevent teachers from leaving. This is obviously much more than any financial incentives actually in place. The effect of class size reduction is also undermined if teachers are not well prepared to work with more demanding students (Paul

Box 5.1. **Directing resources to disadvantaged schools in France, Ireland and Belgium**

In France, *zones d'éducation prioritaire*: Schools are given *éducation prioritaire* status on the basis of the socio-economic characteristics of students and learning outcomes. Mainly urban schools are involved. In 2005, 14% of all primary schools, 21% of lower secondary and 11% of vocational upper secondary institutions were so designated. An evaluation found that the *zones d'éducation prioritaire* had not had a significant effect on school outcomes in terms of transition, attainment and performance of students, and that attending a disadvantaged school may be stigmatising for children, parents and teachers. The student population in *éducation prioritaire* schools has also become more socially homogenous over time because of an outflow of middle class children. Teachers working in these schools are younger and less experienced than those in other schools, and salaries and bonuses for teachers absorb a big part of the extra funding allocated for disadvantaged schools.

In the light of these problems, reforms were adopted in 2006 by the Ministry of Education with the creation of networks called "*ambition réussite*". Under these reforms, institutions will be screened and evaluated more systematically, so that schools will more easily obtain or lose *éducation prioritaire* status. There will be three levels of *éducation prioritaire* status according to the level of school disadvantage. The teaching approach will be more individualised, avoiding year repetition and offering more counselling and guidance, especially at the end of compulsory school. Better progression to higher stages of education will be encouraged through higher scholarships for *éducation prioritaire* students with good results, and through better connections with upper secondary and tertiary institutions. Links with parents and the community will be reinforced. *Éducation prioritaire* students will get help to find a job as they are more likely to face discrimination in the labour market. Finally, teachers will be better-trained for work with these students (through initial education and professional development) and incentives will be put in place to attract them to *éducation prioritaire* institutions (Bénabou, Kramarz and Prost, 2004; Ministry of National Education, Higher Education and Research, France, 2004).

In Ireland, all schools seeking extra resources through the programme *Giving Children an Even Break* are required to respect a set of principles: preparation of a three-year development plan covering school policies to encourage the continued enrolment of pupils most at risk of educational disadvantage and support their retention within the school; collaborative planning with local statutory and voluntary agencies to deliver services to young people and their families; provision of suitable in-school and out-of-school supports for pupils; better deployment of existing resources; new maximum

---

**Box 5.1. Directing resources to disadvantaged schools
in France, Ireland and Belgium** *(cont.)*

class sizes; the identification of learning, social and personal needs and
strategies to meet those needs; better involvement of parents in children's
education; and reporting, evaluation and accounting requirements
(Department of Education and Science, Ireland, n.d.).

In Belgium, two schemes provide additional resources to needy schools. At
primary and lower secondary level, schools receive extra funding if the school
population includes at least 10% of disadvantaged students identified by
socio-economic indicators. Upper secondary schools receive extra resources
if more than 25% of the enrolled population is doing badly according to
various criteria (Kim and Pelleriaux, 2004).

---

and Troncin, 2004). Some countries encourage teachers to upgrade their
practices through special funds for teacher professional development. As
observed in Spain, schools rather than teachers may need to have the main
influence over how funds for teacher professional development are spent
(Teese *et al.*, 2005). To tackle problems like these, in Belgium the achievement
of goals by schools receiving extra resources is evaluated every three years by
an independent body. If a school is evaluated negatively, it loses the additional
resources.

The formal designation of a school as deprived may cause a flight both of
teachers and pupils from that school. To avoid this outcome, one alternative is
to tie funding in all schools to the population mix. This allows for a spectrum
of schools and avoids labelling.

5.3. Defining outcomes to take account of equity

Policy targets for equity

Proponents of policy targets set in numerical terms argue that numerical
targets provide a powerful means of concentrating policy efforts on outcomes,
particularly where national governments lack direct intervention powers and
implementation is decentralised or involves many actors and stakeholders.
The announcement of a target sets a framework, gives precision to a policy
objective, and sets out clear expectations of what should be achieved. Such
targets open leave the means of delivery. They are therefore very different
from policies articulated in terms of the means of delivery such as new
institutions, practices, procedures or legal arrangements intended to achieve
some objective.

A number of OECD countries have adopted such targets for education. In a recent OECD survey, Australia, Belgium (the Flemish and German-speaking parts), Finland, Germany, Greece, Mexico, Portugal, Slovakia, Sweden, and the United States reported that they had adopted results targets for primary and lower secondary schools (OECD, 2006f).

Targets give emphasis to implementation on the ground as well as formal policy and are sometimes combined with measures to increase local or school autonomy. The idea is that schools should have flexibility over the measures they employ and adapt them to local circumstances, but should remain accountable for delivering certain outcomes. Some examples of equity education targets are given in Box 5.2.

Box 5.2. **Targets for equity in education**

- *UN millennium development goal:* Eliminate gender disparity in primary and secondary education by 2005 and at all levels by 2015.

- *EU Lisbon targets for 2010:* Not more than 10% of early school leavers in any member state; less than 15.5% of 15-year-olds in the EU should be poor readers.

- *Government of Scotland:* Halve the proportion of 16-to-19-year-olds who are not in education, training or employment.

- *French- and German-speaking Belgium:* Every 14-year-old student should obtain a certificate of basic education.

- *French-speaking Belgium:* 85% of 20-year-olds should have either a vocational qualification or an upper secondary diploma.

- *United States:* Nearly double the number of minority (Hispanic, black, native American) students taking a rigorous curriculum (Advanced Placement) in 2012 when compared to the baseline of 2005.

Source: Eurydice, 2005; US Department of Education, 2007.

Target-setting has been criticised on the grounds that it distorts practice away from broad but desirable objectives toward more limited measurable goals. Gorard *et al.* (2002) argue that the targets for lifelong learning in the United Kingdom (defined in terms of the proportion of the adult population without qualifications), were met through a redefinition of the adult population denominator. However, for the goal of *inclusion* is particularly suitable to target-setting: while overall objectives of education are debatable, the need for minimum standards – for example in numeracy and literacy – tend to be uncontroversial.

Only a limited number of equity targets can reasonably be set; otherwise they will tend to lose impact. While such targets need to reflect particular national requirements and circumstances, international comparisons suggest two areas – both discussed earlier in this chapter – where countries might usefully consider equity targets:

- First, there are huge disparities between countries in basic reading skills at age 15 and good evidence that school interventions, taking advantage of international best practice, can make a large difference to outcomes. This suggests that countries might adopt challenging but reachable national targets for those skills, measured through PISA results. This is consistent with the overall EU target that by 2010 there be fewer than 200 000 15-year-olds who are poor readers.

- Second, dropout in the late teenage years is a serious challenge to equity. Again, dropout rates vary substantially from country to country, suggesting that some countries may realistically aim for substantial improvements. The EU target is phrased in terms of early school leavers. An alternative way of framing the target, as the government of Scotland has done, would aim to reduce the proportion of young people who are not in education, training or employment.

Targets for fairness are also important, but these may often reflect national concerns, such as the need to improve the position of a particular disadvantaged minority group or redress a gender imbalance.

Schools testing

Some targets and policy objectives can be expressed in terms of administrative data, such as participation and graduation rates. But one key outcome of educational systems is basic skills, typically measured through school tests – typically paper and pencil tests of skills like literacy and numeracy. Such tests can be used for different purposes, including:

- at individual level, to aid the learning of students or to determine selection into tracks and streams; and

- at school or system level, to assess learning outcomes and teaching performance.

If some of these purposes can be realised, the potential benefits of testing are very large. At the same time, the limitations and drawbacks of such tests are widely discussed. They only test a limited range of cognitive skills, and they are a limited guide to school quality given that outcomes also depend heavily on variable school intakes. When the results of tests are given weight in administrative decisions – so-called high stakes testing – they can distort and damage schools' policies. Pressure on schools and teachers to improve performance may also distort and narrow teaching, what some describe as "teaching to the tests", or even encourage fraudulent marking or reporting results (see Box 5.3).

Box 5.3. **The impact of high stakes schools testing in the United States**

In Texas (USA), since the introduction of tests at the beginning of the nineties, the number of students passing has increased by 25% in a six-year period, especially among disadvantaged students. But there is also evidence of perverse incentives. Haney (2001) argues that the improvement in test scores in Texas was made possible by increasing the retention rate of weaker students – a form of student selection for testing. The rate of failure in ninth grade completion for black students and Latinos was three times higher in the late 1990s than in the late 1970s, while for whites the completion rate was roughly the same.

Figlio and Getzler (2002) found that following the introduction of the Assessment Test in Florida, low-performing students and students with low SES were more likely to be classified as disabled (category exempted from testing); poor performing students from high-poverty schools were more likely to be reclassified into disabled categories than students with comparable achievement from affluent schools. Poor schools with lower performance face a higher risk of being sanctioned and therefore tend to be more aggressive in getting rid of lower performers.

To reduce any perverse impact of testing the *No Child Left Behind Act* foresees that for each measure of school performance, states must include absolute targets that must be met by key subgroups of students (major racial/ethnic groups, low-income students, students with disabilities and limited English proficiency). Schools and districts must meet annual targets for each student subgroup in the school, and must test 95% of students in each subgroup, in order to make "adequate yearly progress", and obtain federal funding.

Source: Carnoy *et al.*, 2001; Figlio and Getzler, 2002; Haney, 2001; Skrla *et al.*, 2001.

One possible improvement to raw test scores as a measure of school quality is to allow for the social background of students and so assess the added value of the school in terms of results taking account of the characteristics of the student population. This approach is being pursued in Norway (Hægeland *et al.*, 2004). Sweden has a similar approach but only for comparing grades, not test scores. The grades of 15-year-old pupils are compared by taking account of the composition of pupils in the municipalities and schools regarding gender, foreign background, and education of the parents. England is moving to more complex value-added indicators, which adjust for other pupil and year-group characteristics that have been associated with outcome differences (such as gender, ethnicity, deprivation, mobility between schools, special educational needs, and average prior attainment of year group), comparing individual students with others like them. These indicators have been included in the published school performance tables from 2006 (OECD, 2006g). The main drawback of such value-added measures is that they can be difficult to interpret. This is partly because they are technically complex and partly because they remove effects from the picture which might be challenged rather than taken for granted – such as the effect of poverty on school outcomes.

While standardised tests are a limited measure of pupil and school performance, without them it could be more difficult to compare the performance of boys and girls, poor and better-off children, urban and rural pupils, or different countries and regions – or simply to identify slower learners requiring extra support in tuition. Test results are also an important source of information for school improvement, as teachers and school managers can establish whether standards are being reached and react to different results. In short, such tests are often the "least bad" option available for assessment.

In recognition of the value of testing, in a 2006 survey (OECD, 2006f), most OECD countries reported the use of standardised tests, including Australia, the French-speaking part of Belgium, Denmark, Greece, Hungary, Iceland, Italy, Luxembourg, Mexico, the Netherlands, Norway, Portugal, the Slovak Republic, Sweden, Turkey and the United States. PISA, PIRLS and TIMSS provide key benchmark data on the performance of countries.

Publication of school test results

If the general merits of testing are widely accepted, there is one issue which remains very controversial: whether test data for individual schools should be used privately by teachers and educational administrators or should be published. Only a minority of countries report that they regularly publish test data at school level. These include Greece, Iceland, Italy, Mexico, the Netherlands and the United States. Box 5.4 gives information about practices in some countries.

In favour of publication, it can be argued that pupils, parents and other citizens have a legitimate interest in school performance and in the necessary dialogue on school improvement. Well-informed and open debate on school quality may drive innovation and improvement. Conversely, secrecy can hide weaknesses and remove the pressure on poorly performing schools to improve. In addition, where school choice is seen as desirable, data can guide

---

Box 5.4. **Different approaches to reporting of school-level tests across OECD countries**

Finland: School evaluation information is used mainly to help schools to improve. Evaluation is carried out in a sample of schools. A municipality may pay to have its schools tested. Schools and municipalities participating in evaluation receive their own results alongside information about the national average. The information is not published at school-level.

Denmark: Tests are used to support learning of individual students, but data remain confidential at school level. Each year a national performance profile will be published at national level, so that the teacher will be able to compare the results of a given class with the general achievement level for Denmark.

Norway: The Norwegian national tests are currently being revised. The new system includes tests in reading literacy (Norwegian and English) and numeracy, in grades 5 and 8. Access to school-level results requires a password (available for the respective schools, municipalities etc.).

Sweden: Information has been publicly available since 2001. It includes data on school performance, basic system statistics (number of pupils and teachers, costs, etc.), quality inspection reports, municipality and schools' own quality reports, information on special state grants to particular municipalities and finally added value.

Belgium (French-speaking): National test results are used to improve school quality and equity between schools. Access to information is given to a restricted number of institutions and persons.

Source: Haarder, 2006; Mortimore *et al.*, 2005; Nicaise *et al.*, 2005; OECD, 2006f.

---

parents in choosing schools for their children, either by choosing where they live in relation to a school's catchment area, or more directly by seeking a place for their child in the school of their choice. Competition to attract children, it is argued, will drive improvements in school quality.

Conversely, publication can damage equity if the media transforms even a sophisticated range of data about schools into crude league tables of so-called "good schools" and "bad schools". Public labelling as a bad school can damage morale among teachers, and sap the confidence of pupils and parents, making bad schools worse. In addition, some good schools will have weak results simply because their pupils are disadvantaged. Educated and well-off parents actively seeking good schools for their children and shunning bad schools may reinforce a polarization into good and bad schools, increasing inequity. The evidence in Chapter 3 showing how school choice is linked to increased social separation between schools is relevant.

There are powerful arguments on both sides of this debate, bearing differently in different countries and circumstances (see, for example, Visscher et al., 2000). However, once data are collected and available at school level, it may be difficult to avoid publication. Publication of school-level results may pose risks to equity for the reasons set out above. But modern democratic societies have tended to be sceptical of the idea that government or its appointed experts can be entrusted with information while the general public cannot be so trusted. So the idea that test data should be used by education authorities and school heads and teachers, but not made generally available, becomes hard to defend at a political level. In some countries, including some Nordic countries, freedom of information legislation may make it unlawful to keep such information secret from the public (Mortimore et al., 2005).

While there are arguments for and against publication of school test results, the important issue is how to respond to the test results, as they can provide clear information about equities and inequities throughout the system. Education systems need to plan carefully how to manage and respond to the public debate which will follow publication. But most importantly, education systems need to be ready to give energetic support to those schools with weak results – using the data to enhance equity by bringing all schools up to a level, rather than allowing the pressures of league tables to damage equity by polarising school quality.

In many countries, aggregate increases in educational expenditure will be hard to justify in terms of their contribution to equity although they may contribute to economic growth. This highlights the importance of targeting education expenditure – both across education sectors and across regions and institutions – to ensure that it contributes to equity. National targets for equity outcomes can help.

5.4. Summary conclusions and recommendations

Step 8: Provide strong education for all, giving priority to early childhood provision and basic schooling

Evidence

- Public provision of education can foster equity when it counterbalances poor home circumstances at the outset of children's lives. But it may increase inequity when it provides a common resource harvested by those who are best prepared for it.

- Education expenditure is shifting between sectors in many countries; in some the expansion of tertiary education is a large expenditure pressure. While countries need a high quality well-resourced tertiary education system, public expenditure on tertiary education tends to be regressive; private sources can be tapped to fund this sector.

- Good quality affordable early childhood education and care has large long-term benefits, particularly for disadvantaged children.
- Grants to poor families for school-age children may reduce dropout at upper secondary level.

Policy recommendations

- There is strong evidence that *early childhood education and care*, alongside public policy measures to improve the lives of young children, is the highest equity priority. If fees for early childhood education and care are applied at all, they should be moderate and remitted for those too poor to pay.
- *Basic education* remains an equity priority because it includes the entire cohort. Within this sector, particular attention should be given to efforts to sustain the performance of those with learning difficulties.
- When budgets are limited, public expenditure on *tertiary education will rarely be an equity priority*. Countries charging fees for early childhood education and care but not for tertiary education need to review their policies.
- Countries where *grants to families for school age children* are tied to school performance need to review their policies, since this may in fact encourage dropout.

Step 9: Direct resources to students and regions with the greatest needs

Evidence

- Within countries, regional autonomy in spending may cause disparities in the level of provision, unless it is balanced by mechanisms to redistribute resources to poorer regions.
- Many countries have special schemes to direct additional resources to schools or school areas serving disadvantaged pupils. Such schemes need to ensure that the extra resources are used to assist those most in need and avoid labelling certain schools as disadvantaged, which may discourage students, teachers and parents.
- In many countries, less experienced teachers are working in "difficult" schools.

Policy recommendations

- Countries need adequate mechanisms to *redistribute resources and minimise regional inequities* of provision, so that minimum standards are met everywhere;
- *Extra resources* need to be channelled through schools to help disadvantaged students. This should help overcome the disadvantaging effect of social background, help to tackle poor performance without rewarding it and discourage schools from "selecting out" children from disadvantaged

133

backgrounds. The stigma arising from labelling of particular schools as "for disadvantaged children" should be avoided.

● Experienced teachers are an important resource for disadvantaged schools. There should be *incentives* for them to work in these schools.

Step 10: Set concrete targets for more equity – particularly related to low school attainment and dropout

Evidence

● Numerical targets can be a useful policy lever for equity in education, by articulating policy in terms of what is to be achieved rather than in terms of formal processes or laws. A number of countries have adopted targets for equity in education.

● International comparisons with the best performing countries suggest that some countries could significantly reduce the number of dropouts and students failing to acquire basic skills.

● National testing of individual student performance on basic skills is a fundamental tool to measure both individual performance and the performance of elements of the education system. But test results are limited in what they measure, and results for schools depend on school intake as well as school quality.

● Many countries believe that the publication of results at school level is desirable or politically and/or legally inevitable. A minority of countries are testing but seeking to avoid publication. Some countries are pursuing "value-added" measures of school quality which take account of school intake.

Policy recommendations

● Countries should consider adopting a small number of *numerical targets for equity*, particularly for reducing the number of school-leavers with poor basic skills and the number of early school dropouts.

● Education systems need to plan carefully how to manage and respond to the public debate which follows publication of school-level test results and give strong *support to those schools with weak results* – using the data to bring all schools up to a level, rather than allowing the pressures of league tables to polarise school quality.

References

Bainbridge, J., M. Meyers, S. Tanaka and J. Waldfogel (2005), "Who Gets an Early Education? Family Income and the Enrollment of Three-to-Five-Year-Olds from 1968 to 2000", Social Science Quarterly, Vol. 86, No. 3.

Barnett, W. (1995), "Long-Term Effects of Early Childhood Programs on Cognitive and School Outcomes", The Future of Children, Long-term Outcomes of Early Childhood Programs, Vol. 5, No. 3, Princeton Brookings, pp. 25-50.

Bénabou, R., F. Kramarz and C. Prost (2004), "Zone d'éducation prioritaire: quels moyens pour quels résultats?", Économie et statistique, No. 380, 2004, http://media.education.gouv.fr/file/35/4/2354.pdf.

Building Educational Success Together (2006), "Growth and Disparity: A Decade of US Public School Construction", Building Educational Success Together, Washington, DC, www.edfacilities.org/pubs/GrowthandDisparity.pdf.

Calero, J. (2005), Thematic Review of Equity in Education: Country Analytical Report – Spain.

Cameron, S. and J. Heckman (1999), "The Dynamics of Educational Attainment for Blacks, Hispanics and Whites", Working Paper 7294, National Bureau of Economic Research, Cambridge, MA.

Carneiro, P. and J. Heckman (2002), "The Evidence on Credit Constraints in Post-Secondary Schooling", Institute for the Study of Labor (IZA) Discussion Paper, No. 518.

Carneiro, P. and J. Heckman (2003), "Human Capital Policy", Working Paper 9495, National Bureau of Economic Research, Cambridge, MA.

Carnoy, M., S. Loeb and T. Smith (2001), "Do High State Test Scores in Texas Make for Better High School Outcomes?", Research Report RR-047, Consortium for Policy Research in Education, University of Pennsylvania.

Chiswick, B. and N. DebBurnam (2004), "Pre-School Enrollment: An Analysis by Immigrant Generation", Centre for Research and Analysis of Migration Discussion Paper, No. 04/04.

Commission of the European Communities (2006), Communication from the Commission to the Council and to the European Parliament, Efficiency and Equity in European Education and Training Systems, SEC(2006)1096.

Council of the European Union (2006), Conclusions of the Council and the Representatives of the Governments of the Member States, Meeting within the Council, on Efficiency and Equity in Education and Training, 15 November 2006.

Crouch, D., "School Meals Around the World", 30 March 2005, Guardian Unlimited.

Cunha, F., J. Heckman, L. Lochner and D. Masterov (2005), "Interpreting the Evidence on Life Cycle Skill Formation", Working Paper 11331, National Bureau of Economic Research, Cambridge MA.

Darling-Hammond, L. (2000), "Teacher Quality and Student Achievement: A Review of State Policy and Evidence", Education Policy Analysis Archives, Vol. 8, No. 1, http://epaa.asu.edu/epaa/v8n1/.

Dearden, L., C. Emmerson, C. Frayne and C. Meghir (2006), Education Subsidies and School Drop-Out Rates, Center for the Economics of Education, London School of Economics.

De la Fuente, A. (2003), Human Capital in a Global and Knowledge-Based Economy, Part II: Assessment at the EU Country Level, Employment and European Social Fund, European Commission.

Demeuse, M. (2003), "Réduire les différences : oui mais lesquelles?", in La Discrimination positive en France et dans le monde, Actes du colloque internationale organisé les 5 et 6 mars à Paris, CNDP éditeur, pp. 87-102.

Department of Education and Science, Ireland (n.d.), *Giving Children an Even Break*, *www.education.ie*, accessed 2 March 2007.

Dickens, W., I. Sawhill and J. Tebbs (2006), "The Effects of Investing in Early Education on Economic Growth", *Policy Brief 153*, The Brookings Institution, Washington.

Eurydice (2005), *Key Data on Education in Europe 2005*, *www.eurydice.org/portal/page/portal/Eurydice/showPresentation?pubid=052EN*.

Eurydice, *The information Network on Education in Europe*, *www.eurydice.org*.

Figlio, D. and L. Getzler (2002), "Accountability, Ability and Disability: Gaming the System", Working Paper 9307, National Bureau of Economic Research, Cambridge, MA.

Goodman, A. and B. Sianesi (2005), "Early Education and Children's Outcomes: How Long Do the Impacts Last?", *Fiscal Studies Journal Articles*, Vol. 26, No. 4, pp. 513-548.

Gorard, S., G. Rees and N. Selwyn (2002), "The 'Conveyor Belt Effect': A Re-assessment of the Impact of National Targets for Lifelong Learning", *Oxford Review of Education*, Vol. 28, No. 1, Carfax Publishing.

Grubb, N., S. Field, H. Marit Jahr and J. Neumüller (2005), *Equity in Education Thematic Review: Finland Country Note*, OECD, Paris, *www.oecd.org/dataoecd/49/40/36376641.pdf*.

Haarder, B. (2006), "A Culture of Evaluation in Danish Schools", *http://eng.uvm.dk/evaluation.htm?menuid=15*.

Hægeland, T., L. Kirkebøen, O. Raaum and K. Salvanes (2004), "Marks Across Lower Secondary Schools in Norway", Report 2004/11, Statistics Norway.

Haney, W. (2001), "Commentary. Response to Skrla *et al.*, The Illusion of Educational Equity in Texas: a Commentary on 'Accountability for Equity'", *International Journal of Leadership in Education*, Vol. 4, No. 3, Taylor and Francis, pp. 267-275.

Hanushek, E., J. Kain and S. Rivkin (1998), "Teachers, Schools and Academic Achievement", *Working Paper, 6691*, National Bureau of Economic Research, Cambridge, MA.

Hanushek, E., J. Kain and S. Rivkin (2001), "Why Public Schools Lose Teachers", Working Paper 8599, National Bureau of Economic Research, Cambridge, MA.

Haycock, K. and H. Peske (2006), "Teaching Inequality: How Poor and Minority Students Are Shortchanged on Teacher Quality", A Report and Recommendations by the Education Trust.

Heckman, J. (1999), "Policies to Foster Human Capital", *Working Paper 7288*, National Bureau of Economic Research, Cambridge, MA.

Hoffman, N., M.L. Ferreira, S. Field and B. Levin (2005), *Equity in Education Thematic Review: Hungary Country Note*, OECD, Paris.

Jacob, B. (2002), "Accountability, Incentives and Behavior: The Impact of High-Stakes Testing in the Chicago Public Schools", *Working Paper 8968*, National Bureau of Economic Research, Cambridge, MA.

Kim, T. and K. Pelleriaux (2004), *Equity in the Flemish Educational System: Country Analytical Report*, University of Antwerp.

Koertz, D. (2006), "Limitations in the Use of Achievement Tests as Measures of Educators' Productivity", The Journal of Human Resources, Vol. 37, No. 4, JSTOR, University of Wisconsin Press, pp. 752-777.

Leseman, P. (2002), *Early Childhood and Care for Children from Low-income or Minority Backgrounds*, OECD, Paris.

Levacic, R. and A. Vignoles (2000), "Researching the Links between School Resources and Student Outcomes in the UK: A Review of Issues and Evidence", *Education Economics*, Vol. 10, No. 3, Routledge.

McCabe, B.. and E. Smyth (2000), "The Educational Situation of Disadvantaged Children" in I. Nicaise (ed.) *The Right to Learn: Educational Strategies for Socially Excluded Youth in Europe*, The Policy Press, Bristol, p. 19.

Ministry of Education, Finland (2004), *Equity in Education: Country Analytical Report – Finland*.

Ministry of Education, Russian Federation (2005), *Equity in Education: Country Analytical Report – Russia*.

Ministry of National Education, Higher Education and Research (2004), France, *L'équité dans l'éducation en France: Rapport de base national présenté dans le cadre de l'activité de l'OCDE*, Paris.

Mortimore, P., S. Field and B. Pont (2005), *Equity in Education Thematic Review: Norway Country Note*, OECD, Paris, *www.oecd.org/dataoecd/10/6/35892523.pdf*.

Nicaise, I., G. Esping-Andersen, B. Pont and P. Tunstall (2005), *Equity in Education Thematic Review: Sweden Country Note*, OECD, Paris, *www.oecd.org/dataoecd/10/5/35892546.pdf*.

OECD (2005b), *Extending Opportunities: How Active Social Policy Can Benefit Us All*, OECD, Paris.

OECD (2005j), *Teachers Matter: Attracting, Developing and Retaining Effective Teachers*, OECD, Paris.

OECD (2006c), *Education at a Glance: OECD Indicators 2006*, OECD, Paris.

OECD (2006d), *Starting Strong II: Early Childhood Education and Care*, OECD, Paris.

OECD (2006f), *Public Spending Efficiency: Questionnaire on the Pre-Primary, Primary and Lower-Secondary Education Sector*, OECD/ECO, unpublished.

OECD (2006g), Proposal for an OECD Project on the Development of Value-Added Models in Education Systems, OECD, available on OLIS (EDU/EC/CERI[2006]14).

Opheim, V. (2004), *Equity in Education, Country Analytical Report – Norway*, Economic Research in Norway (NIFU).

Paul, J.-J. and T. Troncin (2004), "Les apports de la recherche sur l'impact du redoublement comme moyen de traiter les difficultés scolaires au cours de la scolarité obligatoire", Haut Conseil de l'Évaluation de l'École, No. 14.

Renaut, A. (2002), *Que faire des universités*, Bayard, Paris.

Rothstein, R. (2005), "The Limits of Testing", *American School Board Journal*, February 2005.

Rouse, C. (2000), "School Reform in the 21st Century: A Look as the Effect of Class Size and School Vouchers and the Academic Achievement on Minority Students", *Working Paper 440*, Princeton University.

Skrla, L., J. Scheurich, J. Johnson and J. Koschoreck (2001), "Accountability for Equity: Can State Policy Leverage Social Justice", *International Journal of Leadership in Education*, Vol. 4, No. 3, Taylor and Francis, pp. 237-260.

Sylva, K., E. Melhuish, P. Sammons, I. Siraj-Blatchford, B. Taggart and K. Elliot (2003) *The Effective Provision of Pre-School Education (EPPE) Project: Findings from the Pre-school Period, Summary of Findings*. Institute of Education/Surestart, *www.ioe.ac.uk/cdl/eppe/pdfs/eppe_brief2503.pdf*.

Teese, R., P. Aasen, S. Field and B. Pont (2005), *Equity in Education Thematic Review: Spain Country Note*, OECD, Paris, *www.oecd.org/dataoecd/41/39/36361409.pdf*.

US Department of Education (2007), *Strategic Plan for Fiscal Years 2007-2012*, US Department of Education, Washington, DC.

Visscher A., S. Karsten, T. de Jong and R. Bosker (2000), "Evidence on the Intended and Unintended Effects of Publishing School Performance Indicators", *Evaluation and Research in Education*, Vol. 14, No. 3 and 4, Multilingual Matters and Channel View Publications.

ISBN 978-92-64-03259-0
No More Failures: Ten Steps to Equity in Education
© OECD 2007

Chapter 6

Groups at Risk:
The Special Case of Migrants and Minorities

This chapter concentrates on the difficult educational pathways of migrants and minorities. These pathways often reflect how the two dimensions of equity overlap: many immigrant groups tend to have lower performance compounded by low socio-economic background. Approaches to overcoming these hurdles include strengthening early childhood education and care for these groups, avoiding streaming immigrants into special education, improving language training and strengthening teacher professional development to deal with multiculturalism. Measures to reduce discrimination in the labour market can also increase incentives for immigrants to obtain a good education.

6.1. The migration context

Migration is increasing. World wide, between 1990 and 2000, the number of people living outside their country of birth grew by nearly half to 175 million (OECD, 2006e). Given global economic inequalities and diminishing costs of transport and information, this growth is likely to continue. Although an important subgroup of migrants is highly skilled, many have low skills and are socially disadvantaged. Such disadvantage, along with cultural and ethnic differences, can create many potential divisions and inequities between the host society and newcomers. This chapter looks mainly at migrants, but also deals with one minority group, the Roma, whose position was important in some of the countries participating in the review.

Immigration policy and immigrant experience varies significantly across countries:

- Australia, Canada, New Zealand and the United States are countries of immigration (Figure 6.1), with immigration policies favouring the better qualified (OECD, 2005k, Table II A2.4).

- In the 1960s and 1970s, European countries such as Austria, Denmark, Germany, Luxembourg, Norway, Sweden and Switzerland recruited temporary immigrant workers, who then settled permanently. Immigration has increased again over the last ten years, except in Denmark and Germany. In Austria, Germany and Switzerland, and to a lesser extent in Sweden, immigrants are less likely to have an upper secondary education but more likely to have a tertiary diploma. (OECD, 2005k, Table II A2.4). This reflects two very different types of migrants – the low-skilled and the highly qualified.

- Moreover in Belgium, France, the Netherlands and the United Kingdom, many immigrants come from former colonies and already know the language of the host country.

- Countries such as Finland, Greece, Ireland, Italy, Portugal, the Russian Federation and Spain have recently experienced a sharp growth in migration inflows. In Spain, the pace of immigration increased more than tenfold between 1998 and 2004 (OECD 2006h, Table A.1.1; OECD, 2005c, Table II A2.4).

In most countries, immigrants tend to have lower educational attainment than native populations. However in Australia, Canada, Ireland, Korea,

Figure 6.1. **Immigrant populations and their educational attainment (2002, 2004)**

All those over 15

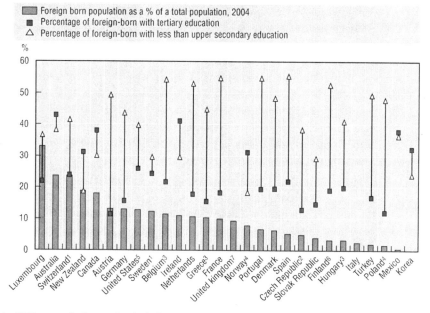

1. 2003 – year of reference for the indicator "Foreign born population as a % of total population".
2. 2002 – year of reference for the indicator "Foreign born population as a % of total population".
3. 2001 – year of reference for the indicator "Foreign born population as a % of total population".
4. 2000 – year of reference for the indicator "Foreign born population as a % of total population".
5. 1999 – year of reference for the indicator "Foreign born population as a % of total population".
6. Less than upper secondary includes "unspecified educational attainment".
7. Educational levels are for people aged 16 to 74.

Source: OECD (2005k), *Trends in International Migration: Annual Report 2004*, OECD, Paris; OECD (2006h), *International Migration Outlook: Annual Report 2006*, OECD, Paris.

Mexico, New Zealand and Norway, those born abroad tend to be better educated. This may be a result of different migration patterns as well as varying educational opportunities.[1]

Discussion of policy towards migrants often contrasts a multicultural approach, which builds on recognition and sometimes celebration of cultural and ethnic diversity, with an assimilationist view encouraging immigrants to merge into a common host society culture. In reality, any clear-cut categorisation of country policies is difficult. For example, France, which formulated its migration policy on an assimilationist approach, has recently given more recognition to cultural diversity.[2]

Immigrants and minorities can face discrimination in their host countries. In many OECD countries, immigrants are more at risk of unemployment and are more often in low-skilled and low-paid positions

(Carneiro *et al.*, 2005; Garner-Moyer (n.d.); ILO, 2005; OECD, 2005e; OECD, 2006i). In France, research has shown that those of North African origin are much less likely to be invited for an interview even when they have better qualifications and stronger professional experience (Amadieu, 2005). Newcomers who are visibly foreign tend to be less welcomed than those whose appearance allows them to blend in (Cutler *et al.*, 2005a; Cutler *et al.*, 2005b; Pitkanen *et al.*, 2002; Alesina *et al.*, 2001). The historical context of migration also makes a difference. According to Schmid (2001), in the United States political immigrants such as Cubans and Vietnamese have been better received than immigrants escaping poverty – for instance Haitians and Mexicans. One implication is that alongside education measures, policies are needed to tackle high levels of labour market discrimination to improve opportunities and increase the incentives to obtain a good education.

In many countries, a broad legal and policy framework designed to tackle discrimination and racism supports efforts to deliver equity in education. In 2004, Finland adopted anti-discrimination legislation that applies to discrimination in employment, education and training. Norway has set up the Plan of Action to Combat Racism and Discrimination, including a requirement for public enterprises to interview at least one applicant of immigrant background in recruitment exercises. France has reinforced its anti-discrimination policy focusing particularly on institutional discrimination (OECD, 2006h).

Box 6.1. **Should data be collected on ethnic minorities?**

Different approaches to ethnic minorities affect data collection:

- Countries more multicultural in approach, such as Canada, routinely ask citizens to identify their ethnic origin, while others, such as France and Hungary, avoid enquiring about ethnic origin as a matter of principle. Proponents of data collection argue that good ethnic data provide solid evidence on which to base policy. Opponents argue that classifying by ethnicity damages human dignity and may lead to discrimination.

- In Hungary, the expert visiting team recommended collecting data on Roma people but on a basis agreed with Roma communities. The team argued that, in the absence of such data, it would be very difficult to help Roma people and to evaluate the results of interventions. In Sweden, the visiting team recommended collection of data broken down by ethnicity, language and religion in order to increase awareness of the needs of disadvantaged groups. In fact, collection of these data is currently illegal in Sweden.

Source: Garner-Moyer, n.d.; Hoffman *et al.*, 2005; Nicaise et al., 2005.

6.2. Immigrant disadvantage in education

Migration pathways

The immigrant experience is highly variable. In the United States for example, while most immigrant groups improve their position with time, some less fortunate groups experience declining health, worse school achievement and declining aspirations (Suarez-Orozco, 2000; Schmid, 2001). In the United Kingdom, education has been a social elevator for immigrant groups, but progress is slower for Pakistanis and Bangladeshis, while immigrants from India equalise their occupational chances with their native counterparts in just one generation (Platt, 2006). Performance can depend more on socio-economic factors than on immigrant background. *The Economist* (28 October 2006) observes that poor, British-born whites are among the weakest learners. In some disadvantaged districts (Barking and Dagenham), the percentage of white children getting good exam results at the end of compulsory school ("five good GCES") is only 32%, lower than that of blacks (39%) and Asians (52%). In addition, immigrants expecting to return to their country of origin can be less likely to invest in new skills which would only be relevant in the host country (Chiswick and Miller, 1994; van Tubergen and van de Werfhorst, 2006; Crul and Vermeulen, 2005).

Participation of migrants and minorities in early childhood education

As discussed in Chapter 5, participation in early childhood education and care (ECEC) is particularly helpful for disadvantaged children. It also provides an environment in which oral skills can be acquired in a second language before learning to read and write. Despite this, in many countries, immigrants and other minorities are less likely to participate in ECEC. In Norway in 2004, 72% of all children aged 1 to 5 participated in ECEC, but among those with immigrant background only 58% did so (Mortimore *et al.*, 2005). Cultural barriers are sometimes involved. Turkish and Moroccan immigrants in the Netherlands tend to prefer to have young children (under 3) at home (Leseman, 2002). Immigrants from Vantaa (near Helsinki in Finland) look at school favourably, but care for young children is considered as a responsibility of the mother (OECD, 2006d).

Performance at school

PISA 2003 provides information on 15-year-old first-generation immigrants (those who were born abroad) and second-generation immigrant students (those whose parents were born abroad). The limitation of these data is that they do not distinguish between different immigrant groups' outcomes. The main findings are:

- First-generation and second-generation immigrant students perform less well in mathematics, science and reading than their native counterparts, except in Canada.

- In most countries, students who use at home a language different from the language of instruction perform less well at school.

- In general, second-generation students tend to outperform first-generation students, but in Belgium (Flanders), Denmark, Germany and New Zealand, second-generation students lag behind native and first-generation students. This might imply a worrying entrenchment of education weaknesses, but it could also simply indicate that more recent immigrants arrived with a better education, perhaps because of selective immigration policies (OECD, 2006e, Tables 3.1 and 3.2).

- Factors such as socio-economic status, knowledge of the language of instruction and the age at migration explain some part of immigrant students' outcomes from education in most OECD countries, but in some countries an unexplained difference in achievement between immigrant and native students persists. As noted earlier, in Sweden immigrant background characteristics do not fully explain the difference between mathematics achievement of first-generation students and that of native students, and in Belgium (Flanders), Denmark and Germany, a substantial part of second-generation underperformance remains unexplained by factors linked to social background. (OECD, 2006e, Table 3.5).

- First-generation and second-generation students generally have higher levels of interest and motivation in mathematics than native students and report more positive attitudes towards schooling, especially after accounting for students' background and performance. However both first- and second-generation students have less confidence in their capacity to deal with mathematics tasks (OECD, 2006d).

This leaves some puzzling questions. Community characteristics, including the cultural value placed on education, are often used to explain differences in educational attainment between immigrant groups – for instance the high levels of educational attainment in some Asian communities in the United States and elsewhere (Zhou, 2005). In other contexts, poorly understood differences in schooling and its response to diversity may be a factor. This merits further research.

Segregation in special education

Some migrant and minority groups are more likely to be diagnosed with special needs and placed in special institutions catering for those children. For example, in the United States, black students are nearly 2.5 times more likely than whites to be identified as mentally retarded and more likely to be identified as emotionally disturbed (Donovan and Cross, 2002; Losen and Orfield, 2002), although Hispanic students are not overrepresented in special education. In some cantons of Switzerland, children with immigrant backgrounds are overrepresented in special education; more than half the children in special classes and schools are not of Swiss nationality (Coradi Vellacott and Wolter, 2004). In Belgium (Flanders), children with foreign nationality are transferred to special education faster than their Flemish colleagues (Kim and Pelleriaux, 2004). In Hungary, about 40% of Roma children have been labelled as "mildly mentally disabled" compared with 9% of all Hungarian children under the age of 14 (Hoffman et al., 2005).[3] However, decisions taken in 2007 identifying individual children as "mildly mentally disabled" are to be reviewed.

Typically, an assessment of a child's ability and behavior determines eligibility for special education. While this may reflect a problem with an organic origin, it may also be strongly affected by the child's environment (Cunha et al., 2005, Leseman, 2002) and disadvantaged children may catch up if they are provided with good quality learning.[4] Potential explanations for overrepresentation of minorities in special education include weaker schooling, lack of knowledge of the language and the school system, culturally different behavior and negative stereotyping (Donovan and Cross, 2002).

Separate streams and institutions for migrant and minority children can be counter-productive. There is evidence that well designed interventions for children with learning and behavior problems, provided in mainstream classrooms, improve outcomes for all students (Donovan and Cross, 2002). Hanushek et al. (1998), in a study of the special education programme in Texas, argued that provision of regular classroom instruction alongside specialised individualised support for students with special needs boosts achievement of students with learning and behavioral troubles and does not detract from the rest of students. Immigrant children with weak achievement sometimes learn faster in normal classes than in special education (Coradi Vellacott and Wolter, 2004). US research suggests that certain minority groups are more likely to receive inadequate services in special institutions and the benefits they reap from special education are smaller than that of their white counterparts (National Center for Learning Disabilities, n.d.). The expert team visiting Hungary recommended abandoning using the catch-all category "mild degree of mental disability" and placing all children in mainstream classes and schools except those who are severely mentally and physically handicapped (Hoffman et al., 2005). In Finland, Norway, Spain and Sweden, special education institutions are reserved for children with serious organic or mental disorders – about 2% of a population (Leseman, 2002). Other children with different needs attend normal schools that provide them with specific aid within mainstream education.

Concentration at school level

Sometimes the concentration of migrants and minorities in particular schools mirrors residential patterns, but it may also reflect the outcomes of selection and choice in school systems. Such concentration appears to damage attainment in some contexts but not in others (OECD, 2006e, Figure 3.7). In Sweden, students in classes and schools with many migrant students tend to have weaker performance and poor knowledge of Swedish. Without special measures to assist learning, a high concentration of students with poor knowledge of the language of instruction may disturb learning.

In most countries, schools attended by immigrant students tend to be in poorer communities. However in Australia and Canada, the schools attended by immigrant students tend to be in better-off communities, and the concentration of immigrant students in these schools does not appear to damage their (very good) performance (Dornkers and Levels, 2006).

The geographical segregation of some minority groups is linked to poverty. In the United States, black and Hispanic students are more than three times as likely as whites to be in high-poverty schools and twelve times as likely to be in schools where nearly all students are poor (90-100%). Such schools may also have fewer resources (NAACP Legal Defense and Educational Fund, Inc. *et al.*, 2005).

Transition in education and labour market discrimination

Students from many minority groups are more likely to end up in low status tracks and streams, be more at risk of dropout, and be under-represented among students in tertiary education. Often social background explains much of this. For example, it largely explains why immigrants in Sweden and Denmark are less likely to stay in school for upper secondary education. Conversely, poor home environment cannot entirely explain the high dropout rate of second generation students at vocational upper secondary schools in Denmark, where 60% of immigrant children fail to complete vocational education compared to 32% of native children (Szulkin and Jonsson, 2002; Colding, 2005). In Norway, transition to higher education is higher for minority students who have managed to complete upper secondary education than for majority students with the same socio-economic background (Støren, 2005). This finding has been corroborated by a study by Fekjaer and Birkelund (2006) that shows that there is a strong polarization in educational attainment among immigrants. Among students of immigrant background, the majority complete only compulsory and/or vocational education. However among those who do complete non-vocational secondary education, many continue to college and university.

Danish, French and Swiss studies show that some immigrant groups are less successful in getting access to vocational programs with on-the-job training. It is a vicious circle. Immigrants are less likely to have a job and find it more difficult to obtain the training leading to a job (Colding, 2005; Garner-Moyer, n.d.; Coradi Vellacott and Wolter, 2004). Such obstacles also reduce the incentives for migrants and minorities to obtain qualifications in the first place.

6.3. Policy interventions

Improving language skills

Immigrant students who speak a different language at home may have weaker school performance (OECD, 2004b; OECD, 2006e) and their parents may be less able to help with homework and less involved with the school. One Mexican boy in the United States persuaded his father that the "F" (the lowest grade) on his report card stood for fabulous (Suarez-Orozco, 2000). In most countries, language training for children aims to allow them to fully integrate into mainstream classes (Table 6.1).

While many newly arrived immigrant children are immediately placed into regular classes (sometimes receiving additional support to develop language skills), others receive language training in preparatory classes before they transfer to mainstream instruction. While this approach may work well, it sometimes leads to problems. In Sweden, children in classes for non-native speakers often stayed there more than one year rather than joining the mainstream class (Nicaise et al., 2005). Similarly, in Norway 20% of students with

Table 6.1. **Language training for children with immigrant background in basic education**

	Intensive teaching of the language of instruction	Bilingual tuition
Belgium (Flanders)	+	
Finland	+	+
France	+	−
Hungary	−	−
Norway	+	+
Slovenia	+	−
Spain	+	−
Sweden	+	+
Switzerland	+	Depends on canton

Source: Eurydice (2004), Integrating Immigrant Children into Schools in Europe, Eurydice, Brussels; OECD (2006e), Where Immigrant Students Succeed: A Comparative Review of Performance and Engagement in PISA 2003, OECD, Paris.

immigrant background never leave the special language training class. To facilitate the transition into ordinary classes of immigrant children receiving special training in Norwegian, Norway has developed a new level-differentiated curriculum and standardised tools for charting language proficiency. The use of the new curriculum is optional for municipalities. In Switzerland, even after two years in special beginners' classes, most children with migration background are still not deemed capable of integrating into normal school classes; they have a lower than average level of cognitive development and knowledge of the official language. Extra funding for separate classes sometimes distorts learning, encouraging schools to retain pupils in these classes beyond the point where it is helpful to them (Mortimore et al., 2005; Coradi Vellacott and Wolter, 2004). By contrast, in Spain newly arrived migrant children who don't speak Spanish typically only spend a few months in separate "welcome classes" before integrating into mainstream classes – apparently without great difficulty.

A few countries pursue a bilingual approach, teaching both in the majority language and in the mother tongue.[5] In Sweden, mother-tongue assistance and instruction in preschool is legally guaranteed, following Swedish research suggesting that mother-tongue teaching improves performance and outcomes, especially in early childhood (Nicaise et al., 2005). However, while 10 years ago, 60% of all multilingual children at preschool received mother tongue assistance, now only 13% do so.

Regardless of the approach, many countries struggle to meet rising demand for language training, in the face of a shortage of qualified teachers specialised in teaching the official language as a second language and a lack of appropriate teaching materials.

Box 6.2. **Swedish programme for Roma children**

In Sweden, through the *Nytorpsskolan* programme, links have been forged between Roma families and the local school through the recruitment of Roma teachers and staff. A special Roma class offers Swedish in the afternoon. Course content is adapted to Roma culture: examples relating to horse-raising are used in mathematics classes and traditional embroidery handicrafts are taught to girls. By liaising with parents, the Roma teachers have reduced dropout to zero (Nicaise et al., 2005, p. 47).

Training measures for adult immigrants

Most countries provide language training for adult immigrants (Table 6.2). In some countries, knowledge of the national language and/or participation in language courses has become a condition for state aid and support. Some

Table 6.2. **Language training for adult immigrants**

Belgium (Flanders)	All new immigrants should attend a compulsory integration programme including language training. Courses are organised in Centres for Basic and Adult Education.
Finland	Adult immigrants receive free integration training that includes Finnish language courses. Non-participants risk losing the integration subsidy. Finnish and Swedish can be studied at vocational adult education centres, folk high schools, adult education centres, general upper secondary schools for adults and at language centres in higher education institutions and summer universities.
France	France's contract between the state and the immigrant (*le contrat d'accueil et d'intégration*) implies that the state provides language training to those who need it. Courses at basic level are offered free to newcomers with low levels of educational attainment
Norway	Immigrants are required to take a language proficiency test and to pursue free training in Norwegian, except foreign workers who must pay for themselves. For all newcomers between 18 and 55, training is a condition for receiving a settlement permit and nationality. The programme must be completed within the first three years in Norway. The right to free Norwegian tuition has been removed for asylum seekers.
Spain	Spanish courses for newcomers are non-mandatory and free.
Sweden	Free training in Swedish is provided for immigrants by municipalities. Since 2006, immigrants may pursue a flexible Swedish language course that can be combined with vocational training and work experience.
Switzerland	Immigrants may participate in language courses offered by vocational schools, communes and private providers. Courses are usually not free but often subsidised by cantons.

Source: Finnish National Board of Education (2006), *Immigrant Education in Finland, www.edu.fi/english*; Kim, T. and K. Pelleriaux (2004), *Equity in the Flemish Educational System: Country Analytical Report,* University of Antwerp; OECD (2006h), *International Migration Outlook: Annual Report 2006,* OECD, Paris; OECD (2006e), *Where Immigrant Students Succeed: A Comparative Review of Performance and Engagement in PISA 2003,* OECD, Paris; *ministère de l'Emploi, de la Cohésion sociale et du Logement,* France (n.d), *www.social.gouv.fr.*

countries also provide broader integration programmes for recent immigrants. In Finland for example, one-year *integration training* for adult immigrants includes language programmes, courses in Finnish society and culture, on-the-job training that allows immigrants to see what work is like in Finland, individual counselling and guidance, remedial instruction if necessary, and preparatory vocational training. Outcomes are apparently positive (Mäkinen *et al.*, 2005).

Sweden has launched the *Skills Assessment on the Job* initiative to facilitate the recognition of foreign workers' skills and credentials. Immigrants are offered a three-week apprenticeship in their profession where they can demonstrate skills they gained abroad. At the end of the apprenticeship, they receive a document attesting to their competencies (OECD, 2006h).

Other initiatives

One of the challenges of teacher training is to prepare teachers to work with children from diverse backgrounds. The review team found that in Spain, despite recent mass immigration, teachers had not received training to work with children having different characteristics and needs. Often they lacked practical experience, and being good subject specialists did not necessarily make them effective teachers. "In schools whose pupils are drawn from 25 different nationalities and where 8 to 10 languages can be heard in the corridors, the question is not the academic standards of a new secondary teacher (for this should be a given), but whether that teacher is able to package his or her knowledge into flexible programmes that recognise diversity of students." (Teese et al., 2005, p. 38)

Particularly where large scale immigration is a recent phenomenon, teachers need professional development to address the issue of cultural diversity (OECD, 2005j). Participation in professional development varies substantially across countries, with high rates in the Nordic countries and rather low rates among upper secondary teachers in Belgium (Flanders), France and Spain (OECD, 2004d, Table 3.11b). Yet students whose teachers participated in professional development on working with students with different cultural and linguistic background obtain better results. A minimum requirement for continuous professional development, linking participation to promotion or recertification and also to school development priorities might be helpful (OECD, 2005j).

While many countries teach civic values and respect for different cultures, it is often unclear how best to encourage these forms of behaviour. Sweden has developed a website, Swedkid, a project funded by the European Union and involving many countries. It links anti-racism, technology and education. Swedkid seeks to characterise and exemplify the process of everyday racism in society. Minority children also receive gender education. Separate groups of boys and girls are accompanied by a counsellor with the objective of encouraging mutual respect and a sense of gender equality (Nicaise et al., 2005).

6.4. Summary conclusions and recommendations

Step 7: Respond to diversity and provide for the successful inclusion of migrants and minorities within mainstream education[6]

Evidence

- Success in both education and employment varies widely between immigrant and minority groups and between different countries.

- Minority groups are, in many cases, less likely than others to participate in early childhood education and care, more likely to be in special education and more likely to drop out or end up in low status tracks and streams.

- For some "visible minority" groups, labour market discrimination is sometimes extensive. This limits employment prospects and reduces the incentives to obtain qualifications.

● In most countries, immigrant students of first and second generation tend to perform less well than their native counterparts in the PISA assessments of mathematics, science and reading, while second-generation students tend to outperform first-generation students. Analysis suggests that much but not all of this is explained by social background factors.

Policy recommendations

● *Early childhood education and care* is helpful for disadvantaged children and provides a strong environment in which to learn a second language. Special measures may encourage participation by the children of immigrants.

● Where immigrant and minority groups are *disproportionately streamed into special education institutions* attention needs to be given to a) the risk of cultural bias in the diagnosis and b) whether separate schooling is in the best interests of the students involved.

● Newly arrived immigrant children often need *special language training*, but funding mechanisms and the approach selected to deliver this training should not encourage the isolation of such children from mainstream classes after an initial period of at most one year.

● Particularly in countries where immigration has risen sharply, teachers need *professional development* to deal with new demands on matters such as second language learning, a multicultural curriculum and teaching for tolerance and anti-racism.

Notes

1. Comparison of educational attainment among immigrants between countries may be affected by different definitions of immigrant population and different methods of sampling used by countries. For example, data for Norway does not account for immigrants with Norwegian citizenship. According to Statistics Norway, "western immigrants usually hold a high educational level, but only rarely change their citizenship. For non-western immigrants, it is opposite – the educational attainment is lower and they become Norwegian citizens more often". (Statistics Norway)

2. For more information, see FASILD, "Plan stratégique 2004-2006", *www.fasild.fr/ ressources/files/plan_strategique/Plan_strategique_2004-2005-2006.pdf*.

3. Numbers for Hungary are approximate, as no official data by ethnic origin are available.

4. According to Leseman (2002), around 10-20% of all young children in OECD countries show learning problems that are rooted in their background.

5. The research does not provide clear evidence whether bilingual teaching has a positive or negative impact on immigrants' outcomes (Leseman, 2002).

6. Step 7: "Respond to diversity and provide for the successful inclusion of migrants and minorities within mainstream education" is included in the Policy

Recommendations and the Executive Summary under the heading "Fair and inclusive practices" (see pp. 9 and 19).

References

Alesina, A., E. Glaeser and B. Sacerdote (2001), "Why Doesn't The US Have a European-Style Welfare State?", *Discussion Paper*, No. 1933, Harvard Institute of Economic Research.

Amadieu, J.-F. (2005), "Discriminations à l'embauche – De l'envoi du CV à l'entretien", Étude réalisée par Adia/Paris I, Observatoire des Discriminations, April 2005.

Borjas, G. (2006), "Making it in America: Social Mobility in the Immigrant Population", *Working Paper 12088*, National Bureau of Economic Research, Cambridge, MA.

Calero, J. (2005), *Thematic Review. Equity in Education: Country Analytical Report – Spain.*

Carneiro, P., J. Heckman and D. Masterov (2005), "Labour Market Discrimination and Racial Differences in Premarket Factors", *Institute for Labour Market Policy Evaluation Working Paper* No. 2005:3, , Uppsala, Sweden.

Chiswick, B. and P. Miller (1994), "The Determinants of Post-Immigration Investments in Education", *Economics of Education Review*, Vol. 13, No. 2, Elsevier, pp. 163-177.

Chiswick, B. and N. DebBurman (2003), "Educational Attainment: Analysis by Immigrant Generation", *Institute for the Study of Labor Discussion Paper* No. 731, Bonn.

Colding, B. (2005), "A Dynamic Analysis of Educational Progression: Comparing Children of Immigrants and Native Danes", *Academy for Migration Studies in Denmark Working Paper Series* 37/2005, Aalborg University.

Coradi Vellacott, M. and S. Wolter (2004), *Equity in the Swiss Education System: Dimensions, Causes and Policy Responses. National Report from Switzerland contributing to the OECD's Review of Equity in Education*, Swiss Coordination Center for Research in Education.

Crul, M. and H. Vermeulen, "Immigration and Education: The Second Generation in Europe", paper presented at the conference *Immigration in a Cross National Context*, Bourglister, Luxembourg, 21-22 June 2005, *www2.fmg.uva.nl/imes/books/CrulVermeulen2004.pdf*.

Cunha, F., J. Heckman, L. Lochner and D. Masterov (2005), "Interpreting the Evidence on Life Cycle Skill Formation", *Working Paper 11331*, National Bureau of Economic Research, Cambridge MA.

Cutler, D., E. Glaeser and J. Vigdor (2005a), "Ghettos and the Transmission of Ethnic Capital" in G. Loury, T. Modood and S. Teles (eds.), *Ethnicity and Social Mobility in the United States and Great Britain*, Cambridge University Press, Cambridge.

Cutler, D., E. Glaeser and J. Vigdor (2005b), "Is the Melting Pot Still Hot? Explaining the Resurgences of Immigrant Segregation", *Working Paper 11295*, National Bureau of Economic Research, Cambridge MA.

Donovan, M.S. and C. Cross (eds.) (2002), *Minority Students in Special and Gifted Education*, National Research Council, National Academies Press, Washington.

Eurydice (2004), *Integrating Immigrant Children into Schools in Europe*, Eurydice, Brussels.

FASILD (Fonds d'action et de soutien pour l'intégration et la lutte contre les discriminations) (2004), *Plan stratégique 2004-2006, Conseil d'administration du 19 janvier 2004*, FASILD, Paris, *www.fasild.fr/ressources/files/plan_strategique/ Plan_strategique_2004-2005-2006.pdf*.

Fekjaer, S. and G. Birkelund (2006), "Immigration and Education in Welfare State: A Multilevel Analysis of the Influence of the Ethnic Composition of Upper Secondary Schools on Norwegian Students' Educational Achievement and Educational Attainment", *Sociology Working Paper*, No. 2006-04, Department of Sociology, University of Oxford, Oxford.

Finnish National Board of Education (2006), *Immigrant Education in Finland, www.edu.fi/ english*.

Garner-Moyer, H. (n.d.), *Discrimination et emploi : revue de la littérature*, DARES, Paris.

Grubb, N., S. Field, H. Marit Jahr and J. Neumüller (2005), *Equity in Education Thematic Review: Finland Country Note*, OECD, Paris, *www.oecd.org/dataoecd/49/40/36376641.pdf*.

Hanushek, E., J. Kain and S. Rivkin (1998), "Does Special Education Raise Academic Achievement for Students with Disabilities?", *Research Working Paper 6690*, National Bureau of Economic Research, Cambridge MA.

Hoffman, N., M.L. Ferreira, S. Field and B. Levin (2005), *Equity in Education Thematic Review: Hungary Country Note*, OECD, Paris.

International Labour Organization (ILO) (2005), *Discrimination Testing Based on ILO Methodology*, ILO, Geneva.

Kim, T. and K. Pelleriaux (2004), *Equity in the Flemish Educational System: Country Analytical Report*, University of Antwerp.

Leseman, P. (2002), *Early Childhood and Care for Children from Low-income or Minority Backgrounds*, OECD, Paris.

Losen, D. and G. Orfield (2002), "Racial Inequity in Special Education" in D. Losen and G. Orfield (eds.), *Racial Inequity in Special Education*, Harvard Education Press, Cambridge MA, p. 336.

Mäkinen, A.-K., N. Niklas, A. Tuominen and P. Ussikylä (2005), "Is Integration Training Worthwhile? A Study of Integration Training Programmes for Immigrants", *Labour Policy Studies 267*.

Ministère de l'Emploi, de la Cohésion sociale et du Logement, France (n.d.), *www.social.gouv.fr*.

Mortimore, P., S. Field and B. Pont (2005), *Equity in Education Thematic Review: Norway Country Note*, OECD, Paris, *www.oecd.org/dataoecd/10/6/35892523.pdf*.

NAACP Legal Defense and Educational Fund, Inc., Civil Rights Project at Harvard University, Center for the Study of Race and Law at the University of Virginia School of Law (2005), "Looking to the Future: Voluntary K-12 School Integration", *www.naacpldf.org/content/pdf/voluntary/Voluntary_K-12_School_Integration_ Manual.pdf*.

National Center for Learning Disabilities (n.d.), *Minority Students in Special Education*, National Center for Learning Disabilities, New York, *www.ncld.org/index.php?option= content&task=view&id=272*.

Nicaise, I., G. Esping-Andersen, B. Pont and P. Tunstall (2005), *Equity in Education Thematic Review: Sweden Country Note*, OECD, Paris, *www.oecd.org/dataoecd/10/5/ 35892546.pdf*.

OECD (2004b), *Learning for Tomorrow's World: First Results from PISA 2003*, OECD, Paris.

OECD (2004d), *Completing the Foundation for Lifelong Learning: An OECD Survey of Upper Secondary Schools*, OECD, Paris.

OECD (2005e), *From Education to Work: A Difficult Transition for Young Adults with Low Levels of Education*, OECD, Paris

OECD (2005j), *Teachers Matter: Attracting, Developing and Retaining Effective Teachers*, OECD, Paris.

OECD (2005k), Trends in International Migration: Annual Report 2004, OECD, Paris.

OECD (2006d), Starting Strong II: Early Childhood Education and Care, OECD, Paris.

OECD (2006e), *Where Immigrant Students Succeed: A Comparative Review of Performance and Engagement in PISA 2003*, OECD, Paris.

OECD (2006h), *International Migration Outlook: Annual Report 2006*, OECD, Paris

OECD (2006i), *Migration in OECD Countries: Labour Market Impact and Integration Issues*, Working Party No. 1 on Macroeconomic and Structural Policy Analysis, OECD, Paris.

Opheim, V. (2004), *Equity in Education, Country Analytical Report – Norway*, Economic Research in Norway (NIFU).

Pitkanen, P., D. Kalekin-Fishman and G. Verma (eds.) (2002), *Education and Immigration: Settlement Policies and Current Challenges*, RoutledgeFalmer, London and New York.

Schmid, C. (2001), "Educational Achievement, Language-Minority Students, and the New Second Generation", *Sociology of Education*, Extra Issue: Current of Thought: Sociology of Education at the Dawn of the 21st Century, Vol. 74, American Sociological Association, Washington, pp. 71-87.

Statistics Norway (n.d.), *www.ssb.no/english*.

Støren, L.A. (2005), "Ungdom med innvandrerbakgrunn i norsk utdanning – ser vi en fremtidig suksesshistorie" in Utdanning 2005 – deltakelse og kompetanse.

Platt, L., (2006), "Moving up? Intergenerational Social Class Mobility in England and Wales and the Impact of Ethnicity, Migration and Religious Affiliation", paper submitted for the Conference on Immigration: Impacts, integration and intergenerational issues to be held at UCL, 29-31 March 2006.

Suarez-Orozco, C. (2000), "Identities Under Siege: Immigration Stress and Social Mirroring among the Children of Immigrants", in M. Suarez-Orozco and A. Robben (eds.), *Culture under Siege, Collective Violence and Trauma*, Cambridge University Press, Cambridge.

Szulkin, R. and J.O. Jonsson, "Ethnic Segregation and Educational Outcomes in Swedish Comprehensive Schools: A Multilevel Analysis", Stockholm University, Stockholm.

Teese, R., P. Aasen, S. Field and B. Pont (2005), *Equity in Education Thematic Review: Spain Country Note*, OECD, Paris, *www.oecd.org/dataoecd/41/39/36361409.pdf*.

Van Tubergen, F. and H. van de Werfhorst (2006), "Post-Immigration Investments in Education Working papers", paper prepared for the meeting of the *Research Committee on Social Stratification and Mobility of the International Sociological Association* in Nijmegen, Netherlands, 11-14 May 2006, http://users.fmg.uva.nl/hvandewerfhorst/PostimmSchoolingRC28.pdf.

Zhou, M. and S. Kim (2006), "Community Forces, Social Capital, and Educational Achievement: The Case of Supplementary Education in the Chinese and Korean Immigrant Communities", Harvard Educational Review, Vol. 76, No. 1, pp. 1-26.

Biographical Information

The authors are analysts in the Education and Training Policy Division of OECD's Directorate for Education.

Simon Field has a Ph.D. in philosophy and social policy from the University of Cambridge and an M.Sc. in Economics from Birkbeck College London. With the OECD since 2001, he has worked on issues including equity in education and human capital and is currently leading the activity on vocational education and training. He is from Northern Ireland. (simon.field@oecd.org)

Malgorzata Kuczera has a M.Sc. in political science from Jagellonian University, Poland and a Masters in International Administration from the University Paris I, Sorbonne-Panthéon. With the OECD since 2006, she has worked on issues of equity in education and vocational education and training. She is from Poland. (malgorzata.kuczera@oecd.org)

Beatriz Pont has a B.A in political science from Pitzer College, Claremont, California and an M.Sc. of International Affairs from Columbia University and was a research fellow at the Institute of Social Science in Tokyo University. With the OECD since 1999, she has worked on issues including equity in education, adult learning and adult skills, and ICT in education and is currently leading the activity on improving school leadership. She is from Spain. (beatriz.pont@oecd.org)

For more information on equity in education, *www.oecd.org/edu/equity/equityineducation.*

OECD PUBLICATIONS, 2, rue André-Pascal, 75775 PARIS CEDEX 16
PRINTED IN FRANCE
(91 2007 04 1 P) ISBN 978-92-64-03259-0 – No. 55657 2007

Lightning Source UK Ltd.
Milton Keynes UK
18 May 2010

154331UK00001B/100/P